For Michael, then and now
—Sis

To the students in my tenth-grade class who
first came up with "an idea for a book"
—Robert

27.00

Burning Issues

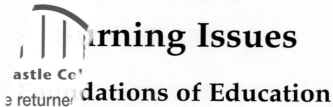

Foundations of Education

Karyn Cooper
Robert E. White

ScarecrowEducation
Lanham, Maryland • Toronto • Oxford
2004

Published in the United States of America
by ScarecrowEducation
An imprint of The Rowman & Littlefield Publishing Group, Inc.
4501 Forbes Boulevard, Suite 200, Lanham, Maryland 20706
www.scarecroweducation.com

PO Box 317
Oxford
OX2 9RU, UK

British Library Cataloguing in Publication Information Available

Library of Congress Cataloging-in-Publication Data

Cooper, Karyn, 1957–
 Burning issues : foundations of education / Karyn Cooper,
Robert E. White.
     p. cm.
 Includes bibliographical references and index.
 ISBN 1-57886-144-6 (pbk. : alk. paper)
 1. Learning. 2. Critical pedagogy. 3. Educational change.
I. White, Robert E., 1948– .   II. Title.
LB1060.C6595 2004
370.11'5—dc22   2004002525

Contents

Foreword

Burning Issues is a rich, multitextured triptych in which each of the three
sections has its own focus yet each is integrally related in creating the
whole. Karyn and Robert have skillfully woven a plurality of material into
this complex work. Each thread adds a new dimension, perspective, and
shading to the whole yet does not lose its own uniqueness. The complex
yet open weave creates multiple patterns as well as multiple openings that
provide, as Karyn and Robert note, "spaces between the theory and the
practice where much learning takes place." This book is refreshing and
thought provoking.

In the first section of the triptych, Beginning with Ourselves, we are introduced to Karyn and Robert, who then outline the underlying conceptual framework of the book. By combining personal experience, critical
inquiry, and social action through an issues-based focus, Karyn and
Robert have created a framework like a trellis that is both extensive and
extending. I found space for my ideas to expand rather than being con-
strained as I imagined myself engaged in the issues presented or alluded
to. In the centerpiece of the triptych, Teachers' and Students' Voices,
threads of bullying, homophobia and diverse sexual orientations, sexism
and feminist issues, diversity and social stratification, and anti-discrimination education are pulled forward for closer examination. The final section, Toward a Pedagogy of Hope and School Change, leads us to imagine more hopeful possibilities for students and teachers in schools. Within
each section and throughout the book, identity, difference, equity, and
context are threads that weave backward and forward, inward and out-
ward to seamlessly connect the personal with the societal, lived experi-

ence with theory, and classrooms with the larger society. Each thread is multiply and contains a variety of diverse perspectives and examples that strengthen the thread itself and the book as a whole. Through multiple examples, this book enables readers to connect and expand their own knowing in uniquely individual ways. It shows rather than tells how to respect and celebrate diversity in a critically conscious way.

Grounding the book in their work with preservice teachers gives it the ring of authenticity, yet it is much more than merely a report of their work. The warp and woof create spaces for learning that go beyond traditional educational frameworks to include broader cultural frameworks. The connection/intersection points bring together materials that lead to new ways of thinking in order, as Karyn and Robert state, to "reconnect teachers' personal and professional lives through a process of critical inquiry." The picture or pattern provides the opportunity for "critical inquiry into self, contexts, and relationships." The inclusive perspective and anti-discrimination stance of this book invite each reader to become part of a pluralistic learning community.

Throughout the book, Karyn and Robert introduce us to a multiplicity of voices from the educational landscape. We hear stories from the perspectives of students at the elementary, secondary, and postsecondary levels as well as preservice and practicing teachers. In each chapter we are provided with stories, journal samples, strategies, and a wide variety of practical classroom examples to use with school students as well as preservice teachers. This makes this book a valuable resource for teacher educators, inservice teachers, and preservice teachers as well.

Margaret Olson
School of Education, St. Francis Xavier University
Antigonish, Nova Scotia

Preface

Schools exist to promote learning in all their inhabitants. Whether we are teachers, principals, professors, or parents, our primary responsibility is to promote learning in others and in ourselves.

—Roland Barth (2002)

Struggling with how to begin, what to say, and how to say it can be a daunting task. What the authors attempt with this volume is no different than what many educators strive for within the confines of their classrooms on a daily basis, as they struggle with complex and competing educational issues. At the heart of this book is the belief that looking critically at a variety of personal and ethical situations may support and enhance inclusion, equity, and democratic practice. But how can educators practice these precepts of inclusion, equity, and democratic practice in the pluralistic milieu of the twenty-first century? This book endeavours to address elements of this complex issue. We believe, as Barth does, that whether they are teachers, administrators, or professors, the primary responsibility of educators is to promote learning in others and in themselves.

OUR STORIES

These vignettes are small narratives from a much larger story of our lived experiences in teaching and learning. They are included here in order to illuminate incidents that are local in context and nature but that extend beyond these boundaries to encompass more universal questions of what it means to teach and to learn, of choice, and of students' and teachers' individual and collective voices.

A Teacher's Lived Experience: Robert E. White

It was raining hard and visibility was poor. Tran shoulder-checked, signaled, and moved into the left-hand lane. He noticed that the car behind him was dangerously close. He sped up. The car behind him sped up. He turned the corner. So did the car behind him. Tran knew then that he was being followed, but he didn't know why. He looked around for somewhere safe. As he pulled into the Hasty Mart on the corner, the car behind him pulled up, blocking his exit. Tran got out of his vehicle and before he knew it, he was lying on the ground, dazed and bruised. A voice rasped in his ear, "Cut me off in your car again, Chink, and I'll kill you."

When I saw Tran at school the following day, he showed me the bruises on his face and chest. His eye was blackened and some of his teeth had been loosened. He told me that the owners of the Hasty Mart had called the police and that someone had reported the license plate of his assailant. Charges were pressed and Tran became a witness for the Crown, as the offense was considered to be a criminal charge.

When Tran received a notice to appear in court, he was terrified of retribution. How safe was it for him to appear in court and identify his assailant? What would happen if he didn't turn up? These and other questions swirled around him, causing much apprehension. I suggested that, if he did not go, his assailant would be freed due to lack of evidence. Tran felt he was a marked man either way.

I said I would go to court with Tran. When we arrived and the case went to trial, his assailant was surprised to see him there. It was as if he had counted on Tran being too afraid to show up. Tran trembled as he gave his testimony. Even though his assailant received only a suspended sentence and a restraining order, Tran was relieved.

As he thanked me for standing by him, he said that if this is what it means to be a Canadian citizen, he was proud to be able to stand up for himself and to see that justice was served. I was, too.

As an English as a second language (ESL) teacher, I came to understand that I was often my students' only link to an otherwise foreign and frequently hostile environment. I tried to provide the empathy they required because I wanted to teach students who wanted to learn, who valued education, and who wanted to be Canadian citizens. I taught ESL because I understood that issues of equity and diversity are uppermost in the minds of many who are marginalized or disenfranchised.

A Teacher-Educator's Lived Experience: Karyn Cooper

I remember grade four social studies. Somewhere between the plants and marine life, I remember being told by our teacher that human beings are part of the animal kingdom. I remember the textbook; there were colorful pictures of beastly looking men with wild eyes, living in caves and scribbling on walls. Our teacher nonchalantly announced that we were *all* really "just animals." There was no discussion. Somehow, I felt humiliated by this prospect. I brooded for weeks. I had many questions. Subsequently, I had many heartfelt conversations with my father about the nature of "humanbeingness." I shall never forget Dad's little laugh when I asked him what it meant to be a human being, yet I always knew deep down that he took me seriously. Being supported in this way was somewhat of a luxury because, for the most part, at school I was seen as an "odd duck" by many of the adults around me. I was often told not to "think so much," to "stop being so emotional," and to "play like a kid." Thus, at school, my questions often went unanswered or ignored.

Much of my time in school seemed to lack a relevant approach, connecting me to the world within myself, where I could find the stuff human beings are made of. I can only now, from the safe distance of adulthood, begin to feel for myself as a child, to remember the hurt of not being taken seriously, especially when the world was so fresh. A pedagogic failure of my own school experience may well have resulted from the tension between my own individual lived experience and the dominant cultural framework on the part of the school. While my home experience encouraged childhood questions of a curious and personal nature, school often mitigated against this very notion, often by disallowing time for any questions. Teachers are often complicit in a kind of hegemony wherein they help to replicate the values of the dominant culture within the society at large. This dominant cultural framework, of which school is a part, often fails to acknowledge that a valid question may begin with the student, with his or her "most embarrassingly general and fundamental questions." Now, years later as a teacher-educator who believes in a democratic curriculum, I envision critical inquiry as an appropriate way to address embarrassingly general and fundamental questions through students' and teachers' lived experiences.

How can educators begin to discuss complex or delicate questions within the confines of their classrooms? We believe that the first step is one of building community in the elementary classroom, through to the preservice classroom and beyond. Building community is a fundamental need, which is not unique to age or maturity.

BACKGROUND FOR THE BOOK

The concept for this book grew out of a preservice foundations course that focused on issues of equity and diversity. We found that integration of lived experience and theory within the classroom and the larger social context of this course were of utmost importance. Frequently, one or two "strands" or theoretical issues are pulled out, examined, and left exposed rather than being rewoven into the fabric of students' and teachers' lived experience. These "strands," pulled out for examination, resulted in the course becoming issues-based. But the issues run deeper than superficial discussions surrounding identity, difference, and equity. In order to successfully integrate one's own personal landscape into the geography of the educational milieu, it is helpful to begin with one's own lived experiences. These lived experiences illustrate what is important to individual teachers in order to make connections among themselves, their students, and the larger society. As a result, this book focuses on understanding how teachers' personal lives influence and inform their professional lives. It seeks to identify, expose, and develop the life experiences that teachers bring with them into the classroom.

Understanding this journey through the lens of critical inquiry, the authors elicit these lived experiences in terms of practical applications for the classroom, both in preservice and inservice settings. This is an opportunity to understand lived experience in terms of a critical analysis of the lived experience of the teacher-in-preparation, through individual life histories and nontrivial readings of the social and cultural location of indi-

vidual teachers. In this way the process moves from experience to understanding the experience to valuing the experience for the purpose of
emancipation and social activism.

ORGANIZATION OF THE TEXT

We begin within the context of lived experiences, situating these experiences in their own personal landscapes in order to move beyond the landscapes into an expression of purpose. Through this expression of vulner-
ability, we seek to address teachers' professionally objective views of
themselves and their work and to articulate a view of the personal, ethical, and moral nature of themselves and the teaching profession.

The book is divided into three parts. The first part, entitled "Beginning
with Ourselves," serves to situate critical inquiry into educators' personal
and professional lives within the context of the individual, his or her experiences, and the effects of these experiences. Beginning with one's own
issues is a frequently neglected aspect of teacher education programs. This
section develops the rationale and conceptual framework for this book, as
well as situating the work within the broader societal context. This forms
the meta-cognitive framework for subsequent chapters.

What does an authentic learning community look, feel, and sound like?
Chapter 1, The Classroom Community: To Feel Safe, questions how educators can begin to discuss difficult questions in a safe teaching and learning environment. What stances can be useful and beneficial in building a
secure and critical environment of learners, regardless of whether the
learners are primary students, graduate students, or inservice educators?

How do philosophical frameworks influence teaching and learning?
Clearly, the notion of respect is crucial to both students and educators in
order to go beyond the "4-D" cliché (dance, dinner, dialect, and dress) of
individual and cultural differences if we are to be inclusive of race, gender, class, and creed, as well as other issues that serve to isolate and alien-
ate individuals and groups of individuals. Chapter 2, Philosophical
Frameworks: Toward a Critical Framework of Inquiry, discusses major
philosophical frameworks for teaching and learning that may be emphasized by educators in order to combine solid theory with practical critical
teaching strategies. The second part of this chapter, Toward a Critical

Framework of Inquiry, describes critical pedagogy in broad strokes. It discusses the need for a pedagogy that is at once compelling and liberating. Introducing critical inquiry into educational practice has many advantages, some of which include 1) teaching students to ask questions regarding their own learning, as well as what the curriculum recommends; 2) providing students and teachers with a voice that is at once emancipatory and proactive; and 3) promoting equity through social change.

Why is a critical framework of inquiry important? Chapter 3, Details, Essential Matters, and Voice: The "Good" Teacher, promotes the notion that emancipation and social change are keystones in the conceptualization, development, and maintenance of a society that is at once critical, democratic, and vital. The second part of the chapter, The "Good" Teacher, discusses how these details, essential matters, and voice may look in practice in a preservice classroom or in a school.

The second part of this book, Students' and Teachers' Voices, establishes a critical awareness between the intercepts of teachers' personal and professional lives. It is the intent of this second section to present situations in which lived experiences are at issue. This cipher for lived experiences will form a bridge between theory and practice, elicited with newspaper articles, poetry, children's literature, educational readings, and other relevant realia. The burning issues identified in this part of the book serve to identify a progression from the individual's own lived experiences to issues of importance for that individual, connecting the personal life experiences to the broader problems in society. These issues will assist in deconstructing teacher identity on the basis of gender, class, race, ethnicity, and the like. Each issue can inform inclusive teaching, learning, and classroom practices, as each lived experience tends to transcend the margins that define it. Each issue may be seen through a multiplicity of lenses that may at once focus on gender, class, and moral issues, to mention only a sampling of possibilities. The construction of students' and teachers' burning issues, with effective layering of complexity and context, is important in meeting the needs of both preservice and inservice teachers.

The third part of this text attempts to move beyond the deconstruction of teachers' work in schools toward a pedagogy of hope and school change. All individuals can find ways to respect and to be invested in those issues that are fundamental to all human beings. To be respectful allows for improved lines of communication in the face of difference and diversity, moving beyond tolerance to acknowledgment and, hopefully, acceptance.

AUDIENCE

While this book provides a framework that is primarily useful for North American and Western audiences, it speaks readily to matters of ethnicity and cultural diversity. Burning issues are chosen to highlight such universalities as grief and trauma. These issues speak to an international audience, as they are reflective of what it means to be human.

This does not mean to say that any or all personal experiences are valuable teaching aids, but a critical perspective can allow a self-selection of experiences that can become emancipating, and may thereby help to promote social and moral activism within the classroom and beyond. Through this book, teachers may be better able to embrace creative and inclusive ways of incorporating the kind of social change the authors anticipate as outcomes for the novice teacher challenged by the pluralistic milieu of the twenty-first century. This book provides a new foundational perspective for education, one that moves away from mechanistic lock steps, providing a way to proceed the methodology of positivism toward a multi-voiced, reflective, and critical vision of education.

This text is designed to not only foster preservice teachers' thinking about their own professional development; it is also written for experienced inservice teachers and for those exploring issues of critical inquiry. The focus on exploring the contexts and substance of one's own history makes for a powerful link between theory and practice. Exploring links between professional development, personal histories, and the contexts and conditions of teaching may serve to have an empowering effect on teachers.

To sum up, we hope that by beginning with personal issues, validating the lived experiences of their preservice students, and allowing for a greater dimension of critical thinking and feeling among their students, teachers can trigger a wider social transformation. This book does not attempt to engage politically correct theoretical rhetoric; rather, it attempts to move critical inquiry into a wider political arena by situating critical thinking and its counterparts, critical feeling and social action, within a postmodern society.

USE OF THE TEXT

This book has numerous applications. It is not intended as a "recipe book" for self-examination and issues-based learning or to provide successful "exemplars," but to situate these issues in reality, in a professional context by which teachers and students work to shape practices and identities. In this way, teachers can explore the people they are, their understandings of themselves, and their experiences, as well as the impact of these experiences in the classroom, the school, and the community.

It can serve as a course book on teacher development, both for undergraduates and for teachers embarking on postgraduate work. As such, the focus on personal lived experience forges powerful links between the theoretical underpinnings of teaching and classroom practices. This book may also serve as a foundational book on coursework and workshops exploring research on teachers and teacher development. As a sourcebook for inservice teachers, the attention would be focused on real lived experiences, theory, and practices associated with reflection and emancipation. Also, this book could be used as a guide and resource for novice and experienced teachers alike, especially for those using qualitative approaches to teaching and teacher development research.

This book could find use in undergraduate and graduate level courses in which teacher-directed research is foremost in terms of relevance. It offers a vision for crafting a career-long tradition in critical inquiry. Teachers may also use this book as an incentive and guide for examining their own teaching practices. Educators of any stripe may find it useful and informative for its provision of art and artifacts, theory and practice, and lived and practical experiences.

In the context of school reform initiatives where, for example, teachers are asked to assume greater leadership responsibilities regarding school governance or for their own professional development, this book may provide a useful guide for teachers exploring sensitive yet under-researched areas in human emotions. It may prove invaluable in developing an understanding of difficulties associated with bereavement, school violence, bullying, and other anti-social behaviours or issues of social justice and equity. It could also be useful for designing one's own inquiry-based research projects and professional development plans. Finally, this book could be used as a guide for teachers involved in university or school restructuring projects.

Burning Issues provides a valuable sourcebook in terms of its presentation of lived experiences, narratives, and other artifacts relating to teachers' experiences and the relationship of these elements to informed positions relative to theory and practice in teaching.

PERSPECTIVE

While our vantage points are somewhat different, we strive to speak with a unified voice that makes clear our individual perspectives. At the same time, while we acknowledge, value, and accept the unique differences of our situations as represented through our differing lived experiences, this situation speaks to the essence of the book: the need to understand difference, the uniqueness of that difference, and the importance of acknowledging similarities that all human beings share, be they children or adults, students or teachers.

The challenge and the invitation of this book is to actively engage educators and students in essential matters—curricular activities that can assist them in exchanging educational scripts that make them uncomfortable for newer, more innovative and inclusive practices that may lead to the development of their own voices.

REFERENCE

Barth, R. 2002. The culture builder. *Education Leadership* 59, no. 8 (May): 6–12.

Acknowledgments

We would like to thank everyone for all their wonderful contributions to this book. In particular, we would like to thank the many students in our various preservice classes over the years for their burning issues. We are inspired that our students have so readily and so willingly allowed their voices to be heard. Many of their contributions are intensely personal, and we are honoured to be able to share them with you.

Also, elementary school students have contributed to making this volume more readable, more interesting, and infinitely more useful to educators at any level of primary, secondary, or postsecondary education. We have benefited tremendously from a number of dedicated teachers and teacher-educators: Barbara Johnston, Nanor Sagherian, Dr. Anne Hill, Dr. D. Pushor, and many others who have helped to bring this project to life.

Our acknowledgments would not be complete without the recognition of numerous postsecondary educators who have contributed their time, energy, and expertise in order to make our classrooms places for whole-hearted inquiry, critical commentary, and platforms for social change. It is the spaces between the theory and the practice where much learning takes place. This seems to be true in life as well as in research.

We would also like to thank the writers of articles in various newspapers for their permission to reprint their words of experience and wisdom, and the authors of professional resources too numerous to name. Many students have also given permission to have their work reprinted in the pages of this book. Thank you to all of you who have assisted in making this book a reality.

Introduction

The more rooted I am in my own location, the more I extend to other places so as to become a citizen of the world. No one becomes local from a universal location.

—Paulo Freire (1998, see ref. on p.17)

We believe the previous quotation from Paulo Freire is an appropriate place to begin. This book provides a study of critical inquiry in action in the hope of sustained school change. There is a need to situate critical inquiry within the field of education to provide a particular vision for a critical analysis of the lived experience of the teacher-in-preparation through readings of the social and cultural location of teachers. Such a stance underpins the intent of the book and provides a strong basis for its usefulness in education today. In essence, teaching balances a predominantly technical endeavour with a socially rich, experientially grounded understanding of its work.

We address the field of critical inquiry through the lived experiences of preservice and inservice teachers. Lived experience—the raw experience that occurs prior to interpretation—provides a deeper understanding of the need to surmount the perceived barrier between theorists and teacher practitioners so that a shift in current teaching practices can be realized. These experiences may serve to broaden and transform other teachers' burning issues, in part by encouraging them to become more rooted in their own locations.

The intent of this book is to provide individuals with opportunities for insight into the value and process of critical inquiry for both facilitating and exploring personal and the professional relationships within the context of becoming teachers. This book will examine how lived experiences reveal opportunities in which critical inquiry challenges teachers and their students to go beyond accepted frameworks toward the development of democratic curricula. By assisting readers to move from a local to a more universal location within themselves and their teaching practices, we attempt:

- To examine the impact of prior experience on the way one lives and acts as a classroom teacher. By beginning with ourselves, we attempt to move beyond "the house of me" to root people in their own locations and assist them in extending to other places to become citizens of the world.
- To encourage participants in greater understandings of themselves, the students they teach, and the broader cultural framework within which teachers live and work.
- To incorporate change for social action. Without the means of becoming agents for social change, "good" teachers may lose hope and eventually leave the profession or remain in their classrooms as merely "mechanical" teachers.

The value of this text resides in its applicability to a variety of school-related contexts and its attention to new directions in educational thought. By attempting to reconnect teachers' personal and professional lives through a process of critical inquiry, we hope that this tremendous potential for social change may be realized, at least in part.

One never really knows what will emerge in a teacher's daily interaction in the school environment. As preservice teachers move into the inservice portion of their teaching careers, they will be confronted with classroom issues that may serve as points of recognition, that may touch nerves, and that may be profoundly disturbing or immensely heartwarming.

This text is about being sensitive to respecting and honouring differences among individuals and groups of individuals. It is about seeking to understand one's own personal history in order to develop a broader perspective from a purely localized one. But how are professionals — preservice and inservice teachers — able to put these precepts into practice? We begin by asking how one connects the personal with the professional lives of beginning teachers in the pluralistic milieu of the twenty-first century.

Part I

BEGINNING WITH OURSELVES

Chapter One

The Classroom Community: "To Feel Safe"

The trellis of our profession—and the most crucial element of school culture—is an ethos hospitable to the promotion of human learning.

—Roland Barth (2002, 9)

We write from the vantage point of teacher educators engaged in the process of formal education. We have often felt a deep sense of alienation on many of the educational landscapes we have traversed. We remember many of our experiences as students in the context of learning to blend in with a voiceless collection of other selves, all sitting in rows and thinking in lines. The teaching practices of the day often subscribed to the notion that silence is golden—specifically student silence. Teacher-to-student communication was often the only kind permitted. Student-to-student communication was forbidden and was discouraged by the arrangement of the desks. We were often isolated from each other.

Even the form of thought in which we were being trained ignored context and made problematic any connection-making other than linear ones. When we did demonstrate that we could bring our thoughts "in line," we were rewarded. Our worth was announced by stars on a chart, but a chart of someone else's making. Every child had a chart. The focus was very much on individual learning, not on learning with and from others. We learned to work by ourselves, for ourselves. The unfortunate by-product of this learning, was, in many cases at least, a profound feeling of alienation.

3

HISTORICAL PERSPECTIVE

As early as 1938, Dewey was suggesting that experiences of both pupils and teachers in the "traditional" classroom were largely of the "wrong kind." He emphasized that the "trouble is not the absence of experiences, but their defective and wrong character—wrong and defective from the standpoint of the connection with further experience" (27). Dewey associates this lack of connectedness not just within the social context of formal schooling but also within the context of education and learning. Interestingly enough, Dewey identifies these "wrong kinds" of experiences as those of both students and the teachers, and that reality has not changed. The high drop-out rate during the first five years of teaching in North America indicates that something is wrong somewhere.

In fact, this theme of alienation is not particular to individual teachers; it connects with much contemporary literature in teacher education and school reform (Cummins 1995; Finley 2000; Freire 1998; Fullan 1999; Smith 2000). These authors acknowledge that the general mode of teacher preparation grows out of research that emphasizes apolitical, objective, and distanced knowing. The result may well be technically correct but less-than-compassionate teaching because teachers are not encouraged by their training to develop the potential for critical inquiry or thought that comes from knowing themselves and others well. Smith (2000) echoes these sentiments when he says, "The plethora of technical and curricular innovations and recommendations under the rhetoric of globalization has left teachers alienated from what their experience has taught them over time, which is that effective teaching depends most fundamentally on human relationships" (18). These human relationships can, however, be fostered in community.

COMMUNITY IN THE PRESERVICE
CLASSROOM AND BEYOND

Over twenty years ago, Sloan (1983) warned of the "erosion of genuine community by a narrow technological rationalism" (238). He called for a "transformation of ways of knowing," cautioning that "the future of the human being and of all the earth now hang upon our recovery of imagination—of a thinking imbued with life and love" (241). Students, be they children or adults, learn better when they feel connected to the subject matter, to their peers, and to their teachers. They also learn greater lessons. They learn not to separate head and heart, the cognitive from the affective nature of their being.

By and large, those who enter teacher education programs, ourselves not excluded, are those who have demonstrated that they have accomplished the goals of "modern" education—the "successful" ones who have learned to remain silent, to think primarily in lines, and to work by themselves, for themselves (Usher and Edwards 1994). If complex and difficult questions around delicate issues about social justice, voice, and democracy are to be realized, then these "successful" ones may wish to reconceptualize "learning" by daring to take risks, to ask uncomfortable questions, to be content in the knowledge that the understanding of complex issues is challenging and often ends with further questions rather than pat answers.

However, if a person wants to teach with heart, with compassion that seeks to ensure inclusive learning experiences, then a learning community in the preservice classroom (and in any classroom, for that matter) is very important. Another reason to be concerned with classroom community is the reality that the larger social community has changed. In the past, societies tended to be homogenous: one dominant ethnic group, one dominant religion, one preferred skin colour, one central ideology. If you were born to that ethnic group, practiced that religion, had that skin colour, and embraced that ideology, you "belonged." Otherwise, you didn't. In recent years, societies have become more pluralistic. Canada, for example, has an official policy of multiculturalism that not only allows but encourages ethnic diversity within Canadian society. As well, the Canadian Charter of Rights and Freedoms forbids discrimination on the basis of race, origin, ethnicity, gender, religion, and so on. The result of these official policies is a pluralistic society of many different voices. In the United States and other parts of the world, too, enfranchisement of previously marginalized groups and changing policies and patterns of immigration have led to an increasingly pluralistic society. To encourage a more global awareness and understanding, it is important that all members of society build and maintain community. Where better to learn the lessons of community-building than in the classroom, a microcosm of pluralistic society? It seems imperative that teacher educators and preservice teachers learn to first build a learning community in their classrooms.

HOW DO WE DEFINE A LEARNING COMMUNITY?

The notion of a learning community calls into question what learning consists of. The "learning" of childhood is often constructed as linear: how to master the "process" to achieve "success" or how to produce the "appropriate" responses that enable "progress" within the society of the school community. hooks (1994) calls this the "banking system" of education, "based on the assumption that memorizing information and regurgitating it represented gaining knowledge that could be deposited, stored, and used at a later date" (5). If this is the predominant model of learning, then there is no need for community. Each student may continue to memorize facts to reproduce on command. The unfortunate by-product of this "education" is the sense of alienation that inhibits all personal development save the cognitive and that ill prepares students for future satisfying and productive lives in society.

If, however, learning is viewed primarily as a complex process that involves new ways of looking at and solving problems and that makes it possible for individuals to function together in a pluralistic society (Edelsky 1999), then a learning community in the classroom is essential, and building one becomes even more so the responsibility of the teacher.

Shaffer and Anundsen (1993) define community as "a dynamic whole that emerges when a group: a) participates in common practices; b) depends upon one another; c) makes decisions together; d) identifies themselves as part of something larger than the sum of their individual relationships; and e) commits themselves to their own, one another's and the groups' well being." Key elements of community are "interdependence, relationships, common purposes, and collaborative decision-making" (Rainer and Guyton 1999, 3). To these elements, Noddings (2001) adds the dimension of caring, or compassion. Compassion provides teachers with the heart to view students as whole people, complete with complex personalities, multiple abilities, and the human need for acceptance and belonging.

Whether the learners are a primary class, a secondary class, or a class of eager preservice teachers, all are engaged in the learning process and therefore share certain generalized characteristics of a learning community. While age and maturity determine the mode and tone of interactive inquiry in a learning community, everyone becomes part of everyone else's learning. A learning community breaks down the old hierarchical relationship of teacher and students; learning becomes an interactive relationship between teacher and students and between the students themselves. In a learning community, the teacher is not all-knowing and all-powerful; students may and can contribute safely to the stock of classroom knowledge from their own experiences. According to Palmer's (1998) model, a learning community "is circular, interactive and dynamic rather than linear and static, and emphasizes relationships among knowers with the subject as the connective core of the relationships" (Rainer and Guyton 1999, 2). For example, through crafting burning issues, students can provide support for each other's learning and development. They can facilitate multiple points of engagement with content by interacting with one another.

Besides students interacting with students for enhancement of cognitive knowledge, a learning community provides for the understanding of others' multiple diversities (Elbaz-Luwisch 2001). As well, a learning community encourages personal growth of the individual. A supportive and caring community provides students with means to succeed in life itself. As Gibbs (1998) points out, communities that foster caring and supportive relationships, positive and high expectations, and opportunities for meaningful participation successfully work to encourage personal growth in individual members because they meet the "basic human needs for love and belonging; for respect, challenge, and structure; for involvement, power and, ultimately, meaning." Thus, while community members identify with the group, they may also be growing in their personal identities and self-knowledge.

HOW DO EDUCATORS CREATE A LEARNING COMMUNITY?

We believe that "community" cannot be created by fiat. While a principal of a school or a chairperson of a department may encourage "subordinates" to create a community, delivery of the same may be problematic. Neither students nor colleagues can be forced to support each other's learning. To do so may result in a rift between what can be said publicly and what people dare to express privately. Thus, the class objective of a truly supportive learning community may not be achieved.

From biblical injunctions to the cultures of many societies, sharing of food and drink is a bonding activity. Providing that it is not repetitive to the point of becoming a cliché, a positive experience for community-building is sharing of food and drink. In a classroom or department where community-building is already taking place, sharing can help that process. Most people are well aware of the community-building that may occur over a cup of coffee.

Another element that may contribute to community-building is the physical environment of the classroom. Some educators spend significant time considering how to arrange desks and tables to facilitate interactive learning: round tables instead of rows, circles instead of lines. However, as helpful as seating arrangements may be, breaking up rows does not necessarily break narrow, linear patterns of thinking or behaving. Although a sense of community does not arise simply because physical distance is decreased, classroom arrangement can assist when other conditions for community-building are present.

Neither does community arise solely through group or paired activities. Students may feel just as alienated working in a group or with a partner as they do working on their own. Far more important than seating arrangements and student grouping is the general ethos of the classroom: acceptance, respect, and caring or compassion is essential for a sense of community to develop. Gibbs (1995) identifies some of the intangible conditions for community-building: attentive listening to one another, appreciation of the contributions of others and no "put-downs," mutual respect, and the right to choose the extent of participation in group activities.

These intangibles represent a major paradigm shift from learning as an individual activity to learning as a social activity where collaboration enhances learning (Gibbs 1995). It would seem, then, that to create a learning community requires relationship-building that may begin with a feeling of safety. For example, for students in Grades 7 and 8 to feel safe:

- is to know the teacher will be fair.
- is to know that nobody will use put-downs in class.
- is to know what the teacher expects.
- means that the teacher will pronounce your name right.
- is to know that the teacher knows who you are . . . like knowing your name.
- is to hope that school is a caring place.

BUILDING COMMUNITY IN A CLASSROOM

An educator's personal warmth can make a classroom inviting. Students, whether they be elementary or graduate students, and faculty may exchange tips, make suggestions, offer advice, give support, provide comfort, and generally do the things that a community and good family and friends do for each other. Difficult issues need not be sidestepped in this environment but may be dealt with humorously, seriously, and compassionately all at once. All students may feel safe because at the heart of this community lies the belief that knowledge is connected to life and to living with compassion.

Educators may use a variety of student groupings in order to enhance community-building. Whole-class activities, group work, and one-to-one communication between teacher and student in the form of reading logs, responses, and discussion groups are but one example. But these groupings alone do not necessarily give rise to a sense of community, although they may help it develop. Group work may take place in a context of compassion and mutual respect, qualities evidenced in what the teacher says, in how it is said, and in the responses to the reading logs.

There is no particular set of teaching tricks and no particular teaching style that may characterize educators as community-builders. Rather, it is who they *are* as human beings rather than what they *do* that makes the difference. Fried (1995) says that of those teachers who inspire us most, "we remember what they cared about, and that they cared about us and the persons we might become" (17). A community is always first and foremost a grouping of human beings.

LIVED EXPERIENCES AS
COMMUNITY-BUILDING MATERIAL

In preservice teaching, the authors endeavour to first create a sense of community within the classroom. Glossing over complex issues, either because of time constraints or from fear of what will happen if they are addressed, does not help build community. On the positive side, greater success in community-building may be experienced when students are treated as people with names to know, stories to tell, and ideas to share. Two examples of what community-building may look like in practice are shared below.

Mahawa's Lived Experience: What's in a Name?

Introducing oneself to others seems to be an implicit act in the process of community-building in the classroom at all levels of education. In beginning any class, instructors usually ask students to introduce themselves. This important first step in building community has become a ritual with which many may never have been entirely comfortable, either as a student or teacher. Mahawa's story (Kanu 2000) presents a poignant account of an immigrant child whose teacher makes a name change because the child's name is deemed too difficult to pronounce. Here is Mahawa's story:

My daughter's name is Mahawa. When we first arrived in Canada a few years ago for me to pursue graduate studies I enrolled her in a high school in the university neighbourhood where we lived, and despite some painful teasing from her classmates about "talking funny" (meaning her West African accent), and "having a different kind of hair" (meaning her kinky African hair), she settled down very quickly in her new school and seemed reasonably happy. One of the highlights of my early days as a foreign student in Canada who had not yet made any friends was the sound of the key in the lock to the door of our small apartment, followed by an animated chat about her day in school and all the things which she and Beata (her new Canadian friend) had done.

On one particular day, however, things were different. She came through the door as usual but instead of the lively greeting I always received, I was greeted in a dull lifeless tone, and no chat about school came forth. I asked her whether something was wrong. There was a long silence and suddenly, she said, "Mom, can we change my name from Mahawa to something else?" "Why?" I asked. "Don't you like your name or is there a problem?" "Oh, I do like my name, especially because it was your late grandmother's name. It sounded cute in Africa but here it seems a difficult name to call and remember. That's what my Language Arts teacher said today. Since she started teaching our class, whenever she wants to call on me to answer a question, she struggles with the name and never gets beyond the first part—'Ma.' Finally, today she asked me in front of the whole class if I did not have another name that would be simpler to call."

I sat down slowly in one of the chairs around the small dining-room table. My mind went back to the many occasions since my arrival in Canada when people had asked me my name and responded condescendingly to my reply of "Yatta": "Gosh, I hope I am able to remember that." I also thought about the many African and Asian students I had met at the university who had disclosed to me that their real names had been dropped for Anglo-sounding names that were familiar in Canada. Hae Ryun (Korean) had been changed to "Helen," Ramatoulai (Malaysian) to "Joanna." Ngombelo (Tanzanian) to "Jack"—the list went on. I had thought to myself, "What an intimate part of one's self and one's heritage to be taken away from one." Trinh Minh-Ha (1995) expressed it better when she wrote about immigrants' cultural transformation: "Oh, the humiliation of having to falsify your own reality . . . to fill in the blanks" (265).

My mind also went back to an article I had read a few days earlier in which a young male white teacher had said in a mixed class of white, Asian, and black students that blood cells brought oxygen to the skin and gave the skin its pink color. The black students in the class had been surprised, because when they pressed the back of their hands as the teacher had asked them to do in order to reinforce the explanation, their skin had remained black and did not turn pink. They later recognized the teacher's statement as Eurocentric, but they did not pursue the matter.

"Mom," my daughter's voice brought me back to the present. "Why don't I just change my name to something else, like Vanessa?" (This is the name of one of the girls on the *Cosby Show*, which she regularly watched.)

"No, my dear. Vanessa is easier to call and to remember because it is a familiar name in Canada and the U.S.A. Mahawa is considered difficult because it is different, unusual and, therefore, 'Other.' Listen, why don't I visit your school and have a word with your new Language Arts teacher?"

And so it was that I came to speak with the teacher who was later identified as a student teacher from the university doing her practicum in the school.

Perhaps this vignette will launch a significant classroom discussion concerning the ritual of naming and the fundamental importance of the personal in building relationships between teachers and students. Students may also be willing to share different ideas for breaking the ice on that all-important first day of class. This book may also launch a significant class discussion on how ordinary classroom practices such as naming carry all sorts of taken-for-granted notions about difference and otherness and about the fundamental human need to be known, to be respected, and to belong. A story of this nature may signal the importance of making the implicit explicit and honouring what the students know about the process of community-building. As one preservice student put it: "It isn't enough to model something; I want to know why it is being modeled in the first place." Mahawa's story not only represents an opportunity to understand and discuss how teaching can embrace the pluralistic milieu of the twenty-first century, it also may serve as a way to engage in critical inquiry about teaching strategies and practices.

Nanor's Lived Experience: "To Feel Safe"

One assignment that may be used with preservice teachers involves having them make a book that tells their future students something important about a theme related to classroom community-building. Through this approach, preservice teachers may learn much about themselves and their fellow students as they also become engaged in thinking about the whole process of community-building, both in the preservice classroom and in their own future classrooms. One of the students produced a touching book about herself that she now uses to introduce herself to her students. The book is called "To Feel Safe":

> To feel safe is to leave a country that is at war and to move to a country that offers peace and freedom. In the 1970s my parents moved from their home country, Lebanon, to Canada. There was a war going on in Lebanon. My parents left loved ones behind and moved to Canada because they saw Canada as a safe place. I was the first person in my family to be born here. I was born on May 31, 1976, in Windsor, Ontario.
>
> To feel safe is to have a name that everyone could pronounce. My name is Nanor. It is an Armenian name. When I was growing up I was teased because of my name. Kids would call me Nanoo, Nanoo. I would always cry and wish I had a normal name like Jennifer or Samantha. But now I meet people who say I have a pretty name. Today, my name makes me feel safe.
>
> To feel safe is to go to a school where people don't put you down. I remember when I was younger and I hated math class. I always failed the tests. One day my teacher told me that he would always be there if I needed extra help. Every week I stayed after school and he helped me with math. One day in math class he announced that I scored perfect on my math test. Everyone applauded. To feel safe is to have people who care about you. To feel safe is to never give up.
>
> To feel safe is to have a normal haircut. When I was growing up my mom would give me the worst haircuts and I would be embarrassed to go to school. But now that I am older, I make sure that I get the best haircuts ever . . . okay okay, I am still working on that one.
>
> To feel safe is to go through a weird phase in your life and have a group of friends that don't make fun of you. To feel safe is to have friends that stick by you even when you do something crazy like colour your hair green. To feel safe is to laugh with your friends until your stomach hurts.
>
> To feel safe is to have a pet. My older brother bought me a cat named Pickles on my sixteenth birthday. Pickles made me feel safe because she came into my life when my family separated. I felt sad and lonely, scared and unsafe. Pickles would sleep on my bed at night and purr until I fell asleep. She always made me feel safe.
>
> To feel safe is to have loving parents. Parents who love you because of who you are. Parents who support you and wipe away your tears when you are sad. Parents who remind you of how special you are.

To feel safe is to have brothers and sisters who make you feel happy. Brothers and sisters who you have fun with. I am lucky because I have two brothers and two sisters. I am the middle child. I feel safe because whenever I have a bad day they are here to remind me that I am loved.

To feel safe is to have a best friend. My best friend has always been my younger sister Tal. Whenever we are together we act silly. We stay up late at night and eat ice cream and talk until the sun comes out. We laugh and joke and tell each other stories. To feel safe is to have a best friend that you feel comfortable with even when it is silent and nobody is talking.

To feel safe is to have a normal car. One that does not break down on you all the time, especially in the Winter.

To feel safe is to be able to look in the mirror (even when you don't have all the things that make you feel safe) and say to yourself "I love what I see."

Learning to teach students is a personal and emotional process as much as it is cognitive and rational. The same may be true of teaching adults; it is frequently a personal and emotional process. Only when the personal and emotional are admitted to the preservice classroom can a learning community be built. The practices of compassion for self and others and of reflection on the meaning of teaching and learning do indeed assist in building a learning community. Such shelters of safety and nurture and self-identity do indeed belong in the preservice classroom and in any classroom. The "right kind" of experience for a preservice teacher may ensure the building of shelters on other educational landscapes.

IDEAS FOR STUDY

The following ideas for study have been developed from our own practices and may be used in whole or in part. It is hoped that they may be a point of departure for development of a critical, caring teaching and learning environment.

1. How can educators model community-building for students by building a learning community in preservice classrooms and in classrooms within the educational milieu? Based on your experience, share an ac-

tivity or strategy, such as a "People Search" (see Supplementary Material) to begin to establish a learning environment conducive to a caring and critical community.

2. Read the picture book *Something from Nothing* (Gilman 1993), the novel *Cowboys Don't Cry* (Halverson 1998), or a book on a similar theme. Can you give an example of an object or an environment that made you feel secure as a child? What properties did it have that made you feel safe? Can this example illustrate something of importance to educators about the desire for a safe and caring school or home environment?

3. What are the elements of a vital learning community that fosters a supportive classroom climate? Based upon your own personal teaching experience or practicum, discuss *why* building a learning community needs to be done, *what* it may look like, and *how* to create it.

4. Imagine a school environment that encompasses characteristics of a safe teaching and learning environment. This environment may be based on elements or memories arising from your "formal" schooling. Based on this exploration, describe what a safe classroom environment may look, feel and sound like for you and for your students.

5. Using Mahawa's and Nanor's lived experiences, discuss how both of these themes are similar. What differences can be observed between the two lived experiences? How can these themes be used to develop an exercise or activity that engages students in the process of community-building?

6. What stances are beneficial in building a secure and critical environment of learners, regardless of whether the learners are primary students, graduate students, or inservice educators?

7. Refer to a quotation from Debbie Miller:

And if you asked me about the importance of creating community today, I'd still say it's everything. But now I know that once the promises are written and signed, the room beautifully and thoughtfully arranged, and the photographs taken, developed, and sitting prettily in a frame, our work has just begun. Real classroom communities are more than just a look. Real communities flourish when we bring together the voices, hearts, and souls of the people who inhabit them. . . . They didn't get it because I hadn't *shown them how.* I'd *told* them to be respectful, thoughtful, and kind, but I hadn't shown them what that looks and sounds like. (2002, 17–18)

Miller goes on to say:

> The best opportunities to show kids how occur in the moment. When Frankie says to Colleen, "Colleen, could you please speak up? I can't hear what you have to say," . . . I can't let that pass without pointing out how smart that is to want to hear what someone has to say. I say, ". . . Frankie, could you say that again?" She does and I ask, "So boys and girls, why was that such a smart thing for Frankie to do?" (18)

Reflecting on these two quotations, describe a practical example of what a culture that exemplifies a climate for critical thinking and community-building might look and sound like.

8. Gibbs (1995) identifies some of the intangible conditions for community-building: attentive listening to one another, appreciation and no "put-downs," mutual respect, and the right to choose the extent of participation in group activities. Design a learning activity that builds on Gibbs's (1995) conditions for community-building.

9. Build community in an elementary or secondary school classroom and use the following group discussions:

   • What factors were involved in facilitating community in your class-room?
   • What factors, such as rules, routines, and processes, may have been helpful in the community-building process?
   • Looking to the future, what characteristics would an ideal school community possess?

As a group, describe highlights of your group's discussion. What questions or concerns became evident?

SUPPLEMENTARY MATERIAL: PEOPLE SEARCH

NAME: _____

1. _____ can demonstrate an example of "wait time."
2. _____ eats liver and likes it.

3. _____ can explain the practice of reflection.
4. _____ can describe a professional development opportunity.
5. _____ can recite a poem for classroom use.
6. _____ can describe three traits of a good teacher.
7. _____ can demonstrate the difference between equity and equality.
8. _____ can define the term "diversity."
9. _____ has used a Venn diagram.
10. _____ can give an example of a "lived experience."

REFERENCES

Barth, R. 2002. The culture builder. *Educational Leadership* 59, no. 8 (May): 6–12.

Cummins, J. 1995. *Brave New Schools: Challenging Cultural Illiteracy through Global Learning Networks*. Toronto: OISE Press.

Dewey, J. 1938. *Logic: The Theory of Inquiry*. New York: Holt, Rinehart & Winston.

Edelsky, C., ed. 1999. *Making Justice Our Project: Teachers Working toward Critical Whole Language Practice*. Urbana, Ill.: National Council of Teachers of English.

Elbaz-Luwisch, F. 2001. Personal story as passport: Storytelling in border pedagogy. *Teaching Education* 12, no. 1 (April): 81–101.

Finley, S. 2000. Strangers in the academy: Beginning professors in pursuit of (academic freedom). *Teacher Education Quarterly* 27, no. 2 (Spring): 49–64.

Freire, P. 1998. *Politics and Education*. Trans. Pia Lindquist Wong. Los Angeles: UCLA Latin American Center Publications.

Fried, R. L. 1995. *The Passionate Teacher: A Practical Guide*. Boston: Beacon Press.

Fullan, M. 1999. *Change Forces: The Sequel*. Philadelphia, Pa.: Falmer Press.

Gibbs, J. 1998. Rather than "fixing kids"—Transform the environment. Sausalito, Calif.: CenterSource Systems.

Gibbs, J. 1995. Tribes: A new way of learning and being together. Sausalito, Calif.: CenterSource Systems.

Gilman, P. 1993. *Something from Nothing*. New York: Scholastic.

Halverson, M. 1998. *Cowboys Don't Cry.* Toronto: Stoddart Kids.

hooks, b. 1994. *Teaching to Transgress: Education as the Practice of Freedom.* New York: Routledge.

Kanu, Y. 2000. *Understanding Curriculum and Pedagogy as Attunement to Difference: Teacher Preparation for the 21st Century.* Unpublished manuscript.

Miller, D. 2002. *Reading with Meaning: Teaching Comprehension in the Primary Grades.* Portland: Stenhouse Publishers.

Minh-Ha, T. 1995. Writing postcoloniality and feminism. In *The Postcolonial Studies Reader,* ed. B. Ashcroft, G. Griffiths, and H. Tiffen, 264–268. London and New York: Routledge.

Noddings, N. 2001. Care and coercion in school reform. *Journal of Educational Change* 2, no. 1 (February): 35–43.

Palmer, P. 1998. *The Courage to Teach.* San Francisco, Calif.: Jossey-Bass.

Rainer, J., and E. Guyton. 1999, April. Coming together—respectfully: Building community in teacher education. Paper presented at the American Educational Research Association, Montreal, Canada.

Shaffer, C., and K. Anundsen. 1993. *Creating Community Anywhere.* New York: Jeremy P. Tarcher/Perigee.

Sloan, D. 1983. *Insight-Imagination: The Emancipation of Thought and the Modern World.* Westport, Conn.: Greenwood Press.

Smith, D. 2000. *Pedagon.* New York: Peter Lang.

Usher, R., and R. Edwards. 1994. *Postmodernism and Education.* New York: Routledge.

RECOMMENDED READING

Gibbs, J. 1995. Tribes: A new way of learning and being together. Sausalito, Calif.: CenterSource Systems.

Gilman, P. 1993. *Something from Nothing.* New York: Scholastic.

Halverson, M. 1998. *Cowboys Don't Cry.* Toronto: Stoddart Kids.

Miller, D. 2002. *Reading with Meaning: Teaching Comprehension in the Primary Grades.* Portland, Me.: Stenhouse Publishers.

Chapter Two

Philosophical Frameworks: Toward a Critical Framework of Inquiry

Freedom
My two dogs
tied to a tree
by a ten-foot leash
kept howling and whining for an hour
till I let them off.
Now they are lying quietly on the grass
a few feet further from the tree
and they haven't moved at all since I let them go.
Freedom may be
only an idea
but it's a matter of principle
even to a dog.

—Louis Dudek (1998)

This chapter is about using one's own life experiences as a starting point for examining personal beliefs about self, teaching, learning, and ultimately about formulating a position about the world and others in it. Critical inquiry and social action form the conceptual framework of this book. We believe that it is possible in practice to go beyond the superficial to include multiple voices and scripts in order to foster understanding. Based on the concept that inquiry fosters understanding, we highlight the role of ongoing critical inquiry about self, contexts, and relationships within and among individuals and groups. Dudek's poem expresses the essence of critical inquiry as both an abstraction and a reality.

As expressed in this poem, critical inquiry embodies the reason for both theory and practice. The principle of freedom is equally as important as the knowledge of freedom. In other words, the principle of freedom may be taken for granted if it remains unquestioned. Of course, not everyone believes that freedom or emancipation is a leading purpose of education, but many of the great freedoms include freedom of thought and speech, freedom from tyranny and injustice, and freedom to learn.

Since education is a function of historical forces and societal contexts, to mention just two parameters, it is not surprising that educators are products of their time. Students are also products of both their time and their heritage. Perhaps the hope lies in the notion that students are living and growing in an era when there is a renewed focus on matters of diversity, equity, inclusion, and freedom.

For this reason alone, it is important to question more deeply the purposes of education in order to ensure that we as teachers are not merely training students to believe in freedom as an abstraction rather than as an attainable goal. The following frameworks may be useful in identifying some of the major views concerning the purposes of education.

THE PURPOSES OF EDUCATION

Our synthesis of four main purposes of education includes the rationalist approach, the practical approach, the progressive approach, and the critical approach. The rational approach stresses the idea that school is meant primarily for rational thinking. It stresses intellectual skills and mind-building. The purpose of a rational education is to improve knowledge. The teacher is seen as omniscient and students are passive recipients of knowledge. The curriculum emphasizes classical studies, reason, and logical thinking in which abstract thought is superior to concrete experience. Knowledge, absolute and permanent, is separated into subject areas. This view of the purpose of education has also been termed the banking model, or the transmission model, of education.

The practical approach to education emphasizes practical skills, such as reading, writing, mathematics, grammar, history, and science. The purpose of education is seen as providing a basic education in which the strongest students go beyond the basics. Teachers are viewed as experts

Table 2.1. Major Educational Philosophies

	Rationalist	*Practical*	*Progressive*	*Critical*
Purpose	Improvement of knowledge	Basic education	Fostering reflective thought	Social change
Teacher	Omniscient	Content expert and citizenship model	Facilitator and guide	Liaison and catalyst
Students	Passive recipients of knowledge	Strongest students go beyond basics	Unique individuals	Focus on the whole child
Curriculum	Classical studies	Basics and vocational	Problem-solving, scientific inquiry, collaboration, and citizenship	Student experiences, social issues, and community context
Knowledge	Absolute, permanent, and divided into subjects	Practical, specific, basic, and vocational	Based on student experiences and interests	Teaches students to effect and manage change

about content and models of citizenship. Knowledge should be practical, specific, and basic. It serves as a preparation for the marketplace, and students are commodified in terms of skill development. This view of the purpose of education sees school as utilitarian, a place where students are trained for eventual employment. The workplace is the guide to the curriculum, and the interests of industry and the corporate world predominate (see table 2.1).

The progressive notion of the purpose of education, as typified in the writings of John Dewey, is mainly interested in the nurturing of human beings. The major purpose of education is to foster reflection. The teacher is seen as a facilitator or guide. Students are viewed as unique individuals — their experiences and interests form the basis for instruction. The curriculum emphasizes problem-solving, scientific inquiry, collaboration, and citizenship within democracy.

The fourth view of the purpose of education, the critical view, is to bring about positive social change. The focus is upon the common good, with the teacher acting as community liaison and a catalyst for social change and self-agency. The focus is on the whole child, and the emphasis is on teaching students to effect and manage change. The curriculum emphasizes and connects student experiences to the community context and beyond.

These four views of the purpose of education are not mutually exclusive domains: they serve to inform a particular perspective, be it historic or personal. These views can allow for discussion regarding the complex nature of teaching and learning, thereby allowing a certain freedom of choice.

CRITICAL INQUIRY AND TEACHER EDUCATION

In the context of teacher education, Schutz (2000) points out that the tools of reason are not neutral skills:

> What we are led to believe about ourselves, what we learn about how we are supposed to act, the ways we are taught to frame "problems" and even the tools of reason that we use to solve these problems, do not simply represent neutral skills but are in fact ways of forming us into particular kinds of subjects. "Power" in this vision does not merely suppress or restrict but actually produces actions and desires. (216)

The preceding quotation emphasizes that the purpose of education is linked to democracy and shared power. As reform efforts suggest, schools do not necessarily serve as places that open teachers and their students to the essential matters of life—the social, the personal, the political essences of their lived experiences. In fact, personal and social issues are often avoided. These are some of the issues that constitute essential matters. Sensitive issues regarding race, ethnicity, gender, death, grief, and other heartfelt matters as well as the positives of what it might mean to live a "good" life are often inadequately addressed.

In education, we believe that teacher preparation, particularly through foundations courses, is an appropriate and important place to address essential matters, given the fact that, in teacher education, teachers' and children's voices have not often been heard in texts that purport to be about democracy and shared power. If current teachers have been selected to teach based on their success within the educational system, how can they be expected to address essential matters that have often been denied, ignored, or silenced in that system?

Critical Theory

There are a number of critical frameworks of inquiry, including Marxism, feminism, and poststructuralism (Capper 1993; Vibert, Portelli, Shields, and LaRocque 2002), to mention only a few. Critical theorists in education are ultimately concerned with suffering and oppression, with critical reflection on current and historical social inequities in order to work toward the empowerment and transformation of others while grounding decisions in values, beliefs, and morals (Capper 1993; Greenfield 1993). Critical theorists attempt to free individuals and groups of individuals from sources of domination, alienation, exploitation, and repression (Brosio 2000; Capper 1993). Because we live in a world that is at once social and structured by societal institutions—that is to say that we live in a socially constructed reality (Fernandez-Balboa 1993)—the task of critical theory is to balance knowledge with critique (Brosio 2000) in order to penetrate the world of things, thereby revealing underlying relationships between and among individuals' (Arnowitz in Horkheimer 1972) awareness of their own lived experiences.

Philosophical Frameworks

Philosophers have long depended on critical inquiry as the main tool for reasoning and attempting to find truths. To this end, critical inquiry has been presented as thinking that relies on skills such as doubting, questioning, comparing and contrasting, and judging. The traditional model of critical thinking, in which the critical thinker maintains an objectivity and distance from that which is being examined, is limited and deceptive since it is impossible to abandon one's lived experiences and one's voice completely in order to be objective. Emotions are vital to the process of critical inquiry (Thayer-Bacon and Bacon 1998). However, critical inquiry need not be reduced to just emotions and subjectivity. When decisions have to be made and criteria have to be applied to help one make the best decision possible, trying to be objective can help one make a better decision rather than being immersed in feelings of fear or concern.

It is not enough to merely *have* the skills necessary to be a critical inquirer; one must also be able to *use* these skills. Critical inquiry requires the propensity and skill to engage in an activity with reflective skepticism. Thus, critical inquiry is both a general and specific skill and can be defined as skilful, responsible questioning that facilitates good judgment because it relies upon criteria, is self-correcting, and is sensitive to context (Thayer-Bacon 2000). Critical inquiry also may include a nurturing approach that takes into consideration feelings and what the knower brings to the knowing by entertaining all views sympathetically.

Critical inquirers also require an appropriate disposition in order to become strong critical thinkers (Thayer-Bacon and Bacon 1998). Dispositions include seeking a clear statement of the question, seeking reasons, trying to be well-informed, and using and mentioning credible sources. Also, one needs to develop intellectual humility, learn to suspend judgment, develop intellectual courage and good faith or integrity, and develop intellectual perseverance and confidence in reason. In this way, critical inquirers are able to look at issues from different points of view, even though no one can be perfectly critical (Thayer-Bacon 2000).

Freire shares with many other critical educators, such as Ennis, McPeck, Siegel, Paul, and Lipman, the belief that it is important to give students a central position of power in making decisions by encouraging them to be autonomous individuals.

A Practical Framework

Critical inquiry does not have a simple meaning, and its definition can be distorted or interpreted in different ways depending on how we construct knowledge (Fernandez-Balboa 1993). It is a process that, at its best, is a melding of both critical theory and critical practice in promoting the process of social action, the product of which may be social justice. Critical inquiry, therefore, within the broader frame of critical pedagogy (Fernandez-Balboa 1993), has the capacity to transform schooling.

A practical framework for critical inquiry has a threefold purpose: to develop both the affective and cognitive domains of teaching and learning; to engage in the interpretation of meanings; and to evaluate the potential of the social structure to empower or disempower individuals (Foster 1986). Thus, one goal for such a framework for critical inquiry is the reconstruction of society based on nonexploitative relations between persons, while a second goal is the restoration of humankind to the "center place in the evolution of human society as a self-conscious, self-managing subject of social reality" (Arnowitz in Horkheimer 1972, xiii–xiv)—in other words, the installation of human agency (Held 1980) over bureaucratic structure.

Critical inquiry is not restricted to specific subject areas; it also concerns attitudes, habits of mind, dispositions, and character traits (McPeck 1990; Siegel 1997). Critical thinking ability varies directly with the amount of knowledge required by the problem. The critical inquirer must understand both the processes *and* the products of reasoning (McPeck 1990).

Critical inquiry can begin early in one's experience of schooling. Perhaps engaging students in a reflective practice, such as beginning with themselves, is a way to introduce them to the process of critical inquiry that is crucial at all levels of education.

Thus, critical inquiry as an educational ideal is a moral enterprise in that failure to take as central the fostering of students' abilities and dispositions to inquire critically fails to treat students with respect as persons and therefore fails to treat them in a morally acceptable way. Education ought to respect all people regardless of race, gender, class, and sexual orientation and should be sensitive to the needs of minority groups. While most would agree that exclusion, marginalization, and oppression are morally wrong, inclusive practices may best be understood in moral terms and justified on moral grounds.

A Conceptual Framework

Pedagogically speaking, then, what may constitute "appropriate" and "effective" critical inquiry? Whose questions are to be asked or which questions matter, to whom, when, why, and in what ways? How do we know which questions are important? Clearly the direction in which the answers to these questions lie depends on deeper fundamental beliefs about the purposes of education and the role that educators play.

The technicist view of critical inquiry values the relationship of learning to the development of skills, inductive and deductive reasoning, and the twin skills of analysis and synthesis. The logical view of critical inquiry has a generative component that includes counterexamples, comparisons, and the questioning of assumptions. However, the broader range of critical inquiry, to which we subscribe, includes all of the above skills but also incorporates attitudes and dispositions along with these skills of critical inquiry. Examples of such attitudes and dispositions include curiosity, open-mindedness, creativity, and other consciousness-raising values or attitudes.

We believe that there is a need to reconceptualize critical inquiry within the field of education and to provide a particular vision for a critical inquiry of the lived experiences of teachers and students. The reconceptualizing of critical inquiry takes teaching away from a purely technical endeavour toward a more socially rich and experientially grounded understanding of the relation of the work of teaching within a pluralistic society. Recognition of the need to encourage students and teachers to frame and ask their own essential questions based on their own lived experience may be a first step toward acknowledging the pivotal role of critical inquiry in facilitating change.

TEACHERS' KNOWLEDGE

In their article entitled "Teachers' Stories, Teachers' Knowledge" (1995), Jalongo and Isenberg provide a framework for the examination of deeper themes and issues relating to teachers' individual lived experience. They maintain that teachers' lived experiences are simultaneously an expression of care for their students and for themselves. Jalongo and Isenberg begin with a lived experience about how a teacher's inner strength had the power to profoundly affect the lives of her students. While this recounting has many traditional elements of a story, it moves beyond storytelling to include reflections on teaching. In this way, the lived experience reminds teachers of their ideals and prompts them to become better advocates for their students. By recording their personal lived experiences, teachers can bring additional perspectives to bear on important social issues, since such experiences have been credited with wielding sufficient power to preserve and transmit culture.

Teachers' lived experiences often reveal several interesting features. They capture and preserve the past and they serve to illuminate one's personal lived experiences while evoking stories from others and reminding people of their interconnectedness. They can connect knowing with feel-

ing, can link thought with action, and make guiding principles more concrete by breaking down the dichotomy between practice and theory
through being simultaneously abstract and concrete. Teachers' professional growth and students' authentic learning do not follow an orderly hierarchical progression: they are embedded in contexts whereby the teller,
listener, reader, or writer delves beneath the surface of the lived experience to examine motives, implications, and connections in order to communicate meanings and explore underlying values. As such, they are often the subject for reflection, discussion, and debate. Four characteristics
that identify a good lived experience are that it is genuine and rings true,
it invites reflection and discourse, it can be interpreted and reinterpreted,
and it is powerful and evocative. Personal lived experiences can be used
as tools to explore the nature of one's commitment to teaching—the connection between personal and professional lives, the despairs and satis-
factions of teaching, and the continued obligation to care for students.

The following section attempts to bring some areas of critical inquiry
to bear on the development of what a critical curriculum would look like
in practice.

A CRITICAL CURRICULUM IN PRACTICE: SOME CONSIDERATIONS

In our class, Karyn begins by sharing articles, such as the one by Jalongo
and Isenberg summarized above, to provide the backdrop for students' understanding of individual lived experiences as they relate to teacher education and broader cultural frameworks. Karyn then relates three personal
lived experiences and uses them to explore structures within school and
society through the use of a Venn diagram (reproduced at the conclusion
of this chapter). Venn diagrams are useful tools for showing how students'
lived experiences in schools intersect with the broader design of the sociocultural fabric.

Figure 2.1 shows a Venn diagram that demonstrates this concept regarding the complex nature of teaching and learning, thereby allowing a certain
freedom of choice. The personal lived experiences shared with the students
are about Karyn's brother's disability and the resulting alienation, a common immigrant experience of her father's name change and the subsequent

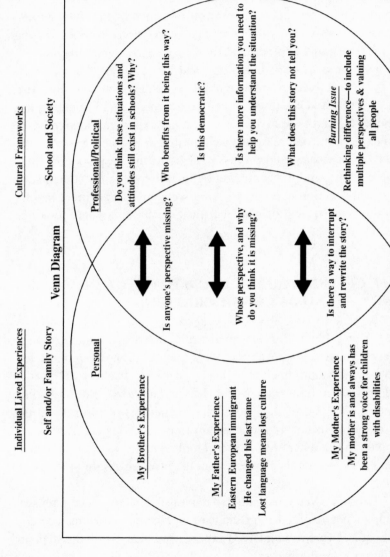

Individual Lived Experiences   Cultural Frameworks

Self and/or Family Story   **School and Society**

Venn Diagram

Professional/Political

Do you think these situations and
attitudes still exist in schools? Why?

Who benefits from it being this way?

Is this democratic?

Is there more information you need to
help you understand the situation?

What does this story not tell you?

Burning Issue
Rethinking difference—to include
multiple perspectives & valuing
all people

Personal

Is anyone's perspective missing?

Whose perspective, and why
do you think it is missing?

Is there a way to interrupt
and rewrite the story?

My Brother's Experience

My Father's Experience
Eastern European immigrant
He changed his last name
Lost language means lost culture

My Mother's Experience
My mother is and always has
been a strong voice for children
with disabilities

Figure 2.1. Personal Venn Diagram

loss of his native languages, and a more hopeful narrative of her mother's activism. The first of these experiences is shared below.

The following lived experience has had a huge impact on the way Karyn views education and teaching. While this may be a personal story, it may serve to illuminate certain cultural assumptions and beliefs embedded within each lived experience. The lived experience shared here is about Karyn's younger brother's disabilities and the school and societal isolation that resulted.

My Brother Enters the Abyss

I loved my brother Michael more than anything else in this world. We were only a year apart in age. . . .

He had eyes of china blue. They were big and wide and sparkled with explosive energy like firecrackers in the night. His hair was yellow and feathery-soft like duck down. He was small for his years. He had a slight limp. His one withered arm was like a little wing that he used expressively, especially when he played soccer. He had a slight English accent like our grandparents. His smile was often mischievously twisted. Yet, he was honest and cuddly and he loved easily.

Then Michael was diagnosed as epileptic. We watched him slowly lose ground. Tying shoelaces and doing buttons became insurmountable tasks. He lost the ability to read and write but not to speak. This is the way I remember my little brother before he was institutionalized.

There are those moments that change a being. Seeing my brother in an institution for the first time, when I was ten, changed my life. . . .

I remember the morning that I first went to see him. The air was crisp with all the dying smells of autumn. I remember being told to look at the trees on the hills, but I didn't like looking at them. They seemed like old withered men dressed up for their own funerals. My mother smoked, dragging all the strength she could muster out of every last cigarette. My father didn't say much, his eyes only watching the road dead ahead. All too soon, we were there. The building that lay before us was Michael's new home.

Feeling anxious and tense, I peered through the window of the car. Michael's new home had high windows and a large front door. There was a playground with one seesaw, the wind whistling a melancholy tune on its pipes.

The door opened and when it echoed shut again behind me I felt as if I'd been swallowed whole. I immediately smelled the stench of urine. My stomach did a quick turn and then adjusted to the assault on my nostrils. There were children everywhere, some wearing hockey helmets or other protective garb. Then a large crowd of them, some young, some older, came pouring around us, pecking like birds, trying to get a tender bit of attention. I wanted to scream but I desperately concentrated on the bare walls. The furniture was sparse; there were a few assorted toys. The attendants had smiles that were starched and as put on as their uniforms.

Then I saw my little brother. Not knowing what to do, I watched my parents. They seemed as small and powerless as I felt. It took me a while before I could focus on Michael's eyes. They were still large, but now they appeared almost too large. They made me think of the vacant windows mirroring the blank expression of the bare institutional walls. Looking at my brother, I felt violated. Part of me was now dead, as dead as my brother's eyes had now become.

This lived experience is a very personal one. Seeing her brother in an institution while she was very young turned Karyn's certainty and security upside down. The policies and practices at that time were clearly defined; her brother was deemed abnormal and no matter how much her mother tried to fight school board policy, in rural Alberta, Canada, there was no place in school for a child with special needs like Karyn's brother. Her brother's institutionalization took place in the 1960s and 1970s, and although there are now more democratic policies in place, one might question how much this story has really changed since that time. Perhaps Karyn's lived experience speaks to values embedded in the wider Western culture regarding the ways in which we treat people of difference or individuals with disabilities. In any case, this lived experience may prompt critical questions and responses regarding the marginalization of certain individuals within school and society.

Certain critical questions are used to focus the discussion on the interplay of individual lived experiences overlapping the broader patterns of cultural social experience. These questions may include:

- Do you think these situations and attitudes still exist in schools? Why?
- Who benefits from it being this way?
- Is this democratic?
- Is there more information you need to help you to understand the situation?
- Is anyone's perspective missing?
- Whose perspective is missing, and why do you think it is missing?
- What does this lived experience not tell you?
- Is there a way to interrupt and rewrite this experience?

This list is not exhaustive, but it serves to demonstrate that real lived experiences blend into the cultural backdrop and need to be revealed in order to examine taken-for-granted assumptions about social cultural frameworks and the school's role in replicating inequitable policies and practices. These questions may provide a useful, transposable framework for numerous applications for the development of a critical inquiry.

As Freire says, "The more rooted I am in my own location, the more I extend to other places so as to become a citizen of the world. No one becomes local from a universal location" (Freire 1998, 39). The authors believe, as Freire does, that it is difficult to get at a deeper understanding of the world without beginning close to home, with oneself and one's own preconceptions. In order to accomplish this, each student may wish to examine his/her own lived experience, the result of which is often a burning issue that is central to the pedagogy of hope and school change.

IDEAS FOR STUDY

Based on some of the concepts presented in this chapter, the following questions and exercises focus on the development of a personal philosophy of education.

1. What would each of the four views of education presented in the major educational philosophies template (table 2.1) look like in practice

from the perspective of each of the following: the purpose, the teacher, the students, the curriculum, and the knowledge?

2. Use examples from your practicum experience or choose a quotation or short verse to illustrate the various perspectives described in question 1. Concrete examples or artifacts contribute to your developing philosophy of education.

3. Using the major educational philosophies template, create a list by adding or deleting items that either reinforce or compromise your idea of what the major purpose of education is for you.

4. Using the list that you have created in question 3, draft a personal philosophy of education. Include a statement about the roles and responsibilities of the community, the teacher, and the students. What would that philosophy look, sound, and feel like in practice?

5. What opportunities or experiences would assist students at any level of education in becoming more critically aware of the school and community within which they live and teach, and of the roles that they assume within these environments?

6. Authors such as Jalongo and Isenberg (1995) provide a theoretical basis and a professional insight as to why it is important to first begin with ourselves. Although Jalongo and Isenberg refer to individual experiences as "narratives" or "teacher stories," these terms, for the purposes of this book, are interchangeable with the term "lived experience." Discuss how lived experiences can inform future directions in teaching practice.

7. Certain critical questions may be used to focus discussion on the interplay of individual lived experiences that overlap with the broader patterns of cultural social experience. These questions include:

- Do you think these situations and attitudes still exist in schools? Why?
- Who benefits from it being this way?
- Is this democratic?
- Is there more information you need to help you to understand the situation?
- Is anyone's perspective missing?
- Whose perspective is missing, and why do you think it is missing?

- What does this narrative not tell you?
- Is there a way to interrupt and rewrite this narrative?

Using the example in this chapter and the template in the Supplementary Material, create a Venn diagram that reveals an individual lived experience using the questions included above. Are there any unasked questions that need to be raised? Students may volunteer to share their diagrams.

SUPPLEMENTARY MATERIAL

See the diagram in figure 2.2.

REFERENCES

Brosio, R. 2000. *Philosophical Scaffolding for the Construction of Critical Democratic Education*. New York: Peter Lang.

Capper, C. 1993. Educational administration in a pluralistic society: A multiparadigm approach. In *Educational Administration in a Pluralistic Society*, ed. C. Capper, 7–35. New York: SUNY Press.

Dudek, L. 1998. Freedom. In *The Poetry of Louis Dudek*. Ottawa: The Golden Dog.

Fernandez-Balboa, J. 1993. Critical pedagogy: Making critical thinking *really* critical. *Analytic Teaching* 13, no. 2: 61–72.

Freire, P. 1998. *Politics and Education*. Trans. P. L. Wong. Los Angeles: UCLA Latin American Center Publications.

Foster, W. 1986. *Paradigms and Promises: New Approaches to Educational Administration*. Buffalo, N.Y.: Prometheus Books.

Greenfield, W. 1993. Articulating values and ethics in administrator preparation. In *Educational Administration in a Pluralistic Society*, ed. C. Capper, 267–287. Albany, N.Y.: SUNY Press.

Held, D. 1980. *Introduction to Critical Theory*. Berkeley: University of California Press.

Horkheimer, M. 1972. *Critical Theory*. New York: Herder and Herder.

Jalongo M. R., and J. P. Isenberg. 1995. *Teachers' Stories: From Personal Narrative to Professional Insight*. San Francisco: Jossey-Bass Publishers.

McPeck, J. 1990. *Teaching Critical Thinking*. New York: Routledge.

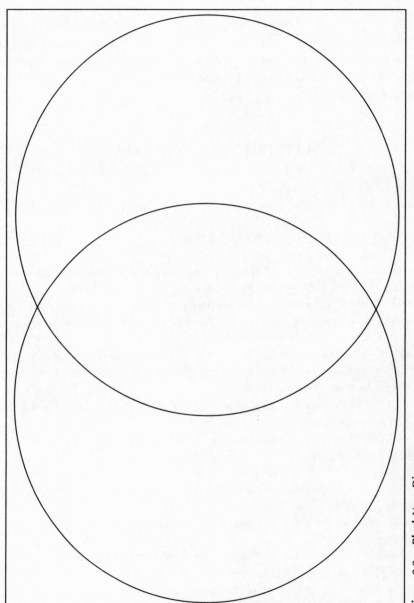

Figure 2.2.　Blank Venn Diagram

Schutz, A. 2000. Teaching freedom? Postmodern perspectives. *Review of Educational Research*, 70, no. 2 (Summer): 215–251.

Siegel, H. 1997. *Rationality Redeemed? Further Dialogues on an Educational Ideal*. New York: Routledge.

Thayer-Bacon, B. J. 2000. *Transforming Critical Thinking*. New York: Teachers College Press.

Thayer-Bacon, B. J., and C. S. Bacon. 1998. *Philosophy Applied to Education: Nurturing a Democratic Community within a Classroom*. Upper Saddle River, N.J.: Merrill.

Vibert, A. B., J. B. Portelli, C. Shields, and L. LaRocque. 2002. Critical practice in elementary schools: Voice, community and curriculum of life. *Journal of Educational Change* 3, no. 2 (June): 93–106.

RECOMMENDED READING

Brosio, R. 2000. *Philosophical Scaffolding for the Construction of Critical Democratic Education*. New York: Peter Lang.

Dewey, J. 1966. *Democracy and Education: An Introduction to the Philosophy of Education*. New York: Free Press.

Elbaz-Luwisch, F. 2001. Personal story as passport: Storytelling in border pedagogy. *Teaching Education* 12, no. 1 (April): 81–101.

Freire, P. 1998. *Politics and Education*. Trans. P. L. Wong. Los Angeles: UCLA Latin American Center Publications.

Freire, P. 1968. *Pedagogy of the Oppressed*. New York: Herder and Herder.

Fried, R. L. 2001. *The Passionate Learner: How Teachers and Parents Can Help Children Reclaim the Joy of Discovery*. Boston: Beacon Press.

Jalongo, M., and J. Isenberg. 1995. How narrative connects. In *Teachers' Stories: From Personal Narrative to Professional Insight*, ed. M. R. Jalongo, J. P. Isenberg, and G. Gerbracht. San Francisco: Jossey-Bass.

Meier, D. 1995. It's academic: Why kids don't want to be "well-educated." In *The Power of Their Ideas*, 161–171. Boston: Beacon Press.

Noddings, N. 2001. Care and coercion in school reform. *Journal of Educational Change* 2, no. 1 (February): 35–43.

Chapter Three

Details, Essential Matters, and Voice: The "Good" Teacher

If I have told you these details about the asteroid, and made a note of its number for you, it is on account of the grownups and their ways. Grownups love figures. When you tell them that you have made a new friend, they never ask you any questions about essential matters. They never say to you, "What does his voice sound like? What games does he like best? Does he collect butterflies?" Instead, they demand: "How old is he? How many brothers has he? How much does he weigh? How much money does his father make?" Only from the figure do they think they have learned anything about him. . . . They are like that. One must not hold it against them. Children should always show great forbearance toward grown up people.

—Saint-Exupery (1943, 17–18)

Saint-Exupery's Little Prince reminds us that our own childhood experiences are registered and understood against those of adults and that these details are framed and interpreted within schools and societies. Acknowledgment of the child's voice and perspective is integral to an understanding of teaching and learning. Therefore this book begins by asking teachers to begin with themselves—to begin not with an examination of adult teaching practices but with recollections of their own early lived experiences as learners. These lived experiences may be rich in details, essential matters, and voices that need to be at once heard, listened to, and considered in terms of relevance to students' and teachers' actual lives.

BARBARA'S LIVED EXPERIENCE

Barbara, a preservice teacher candidate, recollects an early lived experience of schooling. She entitles her recollection "A Blue Bird":

> The occasion when I was bad in class still remains with me. My punishment was innovative. To kneel in a praying position on the heat register located at the back of the class. The register was about 36 inches high and about the same in length. Another boy shared in the punishment. We climbed up, not knowing. We positioned our knees on the grate and prayed. After a while, we squirmed. Noticing that I had moved slightly off the grill, the teacher made me redo the punishment over recess. I had difficulty not moving, so I again tried over part of the lunch hour. I had ample time to reflect. Of course, not everyone had these types of experiences in class. Red birds were too smart to get into trouble. Blue birds only occasionally. Yellow birds were the real bad ones.

What are some of the essential details about Barbara's lived experience? How might this experience impact upon Barbara as a teacher? What seems to be essential about this lived experience as it relates to teaching in the first decades of the twenty-first century?

On reflecting upon this lived experience, Barbara said that she felt there was a definite need for structure and that this experience instilled in her the "virtues" of routine. Although she felt that it was important to "know the rules" and to play by them, she acknowledges that:

> I became afraid to have my own thoughts and ideas. Somehow they were not good enough, or right. I had difficulty speaking in class and would not like to hand in projects or show my work unless somehow I knew it was perfect. Surprisingly, I had erased most of my childhood memories of school and had difficulty remembering a positive or negative experience. The experience, as I look at it as an adult, gives me the shivers.

Barbara puts this lived experience into the context of her school experience. She notes that learning seemed to exist within a vacuum:

> I don't remember seeing anyone else's work in class. We did not share our information or ideas or feelings. Projects were handed back in order by percentage or grade starting from the top. It seemed to be an inefficient way of learning. It was direct transmission learning. The answers were either right or wrong; there were no grey areas.

She remembers taking turns reading aloud in language arts class—one paragraph to each student. She remembers how painful it was to listen to students who struggled so hard. This event has had a major impact on Barbara's philosophy of teaching and learning. It has helped to provide a more critical perspective in her daily teaching practice:

> Being fair is important to me. Giving each student some time and attention no matter what level they are at is important to me. I do not like the idea of forcing someone to do something. I don't like teachers who single students out to make the class or the student feel stupid. I would like to break down the inhibitions and fear of making mistakes and lighten the consequences of some actions that were made with no malicious intent.

This lived experience, even though it was not a positive experience, has encouraged Barbara to develop a direct positive relationship between her philosophy of teaching and learning and her daily instructional practice. She says:

> I like giving lots of examples, sharing stories, setting up a situation so that everyone can win. I like teaching through guided discovery. I like having students try a variety of ways to accomplish goals, allowing them to pick and make decisions, and then practice. I do not mind holding someone's hand until they feel confident [enough] to do it on their own. No matter how silly it may seem to someone watching. I love to give others confidence to do the best job, to create the best possible learning environment and allow the learner in everyone to "sparkle" with interest.

Barbara's lived experience reveals a graphic example of a fundamental universal need—the need for respect.

PHEUNG'S LIVED EXPERIENCE

In comparison to Barbara's lived experience, Pheung, another preservice student, recalls a lived experience from his time as an elementary school student:

> I can remember clearly a specific moment in art period during my year as a fourth grade student. Mr. S. asked us to draw a picture of a person's face. He

held up a picture completed by one of his students the previous year. As I gazed at the drawing, I was impressed by the detail and clarity. It looked very much like the original cover on the magazine. Finally, we were given instructions on how to begin our own "Masterpiece." As I was consumed in my work, I heard my name mentioned in conversation. I looked up and saw John telling Mr. S. that I was using the wrong method or style of drawing. The room became silent. I looked toward Mr. S's desk to see what was happening. I could see John and Mr. S. talking but I could not make out what they were saying to each other. Mr. S. then turned and looked directly at me. I automatically looked down at my work. (In my culture, when one thinks he or she has done something wrong or has broken a rule, when confronted we are not allowed to look into the eyes of our authoritative model because it is considered disrespectful.) So I did not look up because Mr. S. was my teacher. I was afraid and petrified when I saw Mr. S. get out of his chair from behind his "mighty" desk. Finally, Mr. S. was at my desk and I was waiting to hear the word, "Wrong." Mr. S. asked me if I knew what I was doing. I told him, "No." Putting his hand on my left shoulder, he called the whole class to attention. Mr. S. then explained to the class that I was using a method called sketching. He told me that I was doing an excellent job and to keep up the good work.

In describing his lived experience, Pheung identifies two forms of lived experiences or narratives that operate simultaneously (Crites 1971), carrying cultural aspects of experience forward. They are reciprocally influential, because individual lived experiences overlap into the broader patterns of cultural social experience. Western cultural attitudes embody taken-for-granted attitudes that are determined by the way social context is presented and represents the contextual shapes within which individual lived experiences unfold. An individual's lived experience furnishes the opportunity to examine what has been culturally constructed in an implicit way through the cultural experience.

Barbara's and Pheung's lived experiences point to Western cultural attitudes regarding respect. Typically in Western culture, there is a power differential between adults and children. Pheung was fortunate enough to have a teacher who viewed him as a human being deserving of respect. Barbara's teacher enforced her respect for the rules through the exercising of a power differential invested in the role of being a teacher. These lived experiences underscore a basic inherent inequity regarding the status of children within the general social culture.

Perhaps these lived experiences illustrate the issue of respect, an essential matter, the details of which are difficult to teach within and beyond teacher preparation programs. What assumptions can be identified and critically examined in these two lived experiences? In contrast to Barbara's lived experience, Pheung received the understanding and validation that he needed, the result of which was respect for the student and his effort. Encouraging student teachers to begin with their own lived experiences, to listen to and learn from their own and each others' narratives, as Barbara and Pheung have done, to reflect on these and to share them, are necessary practices in developing respectful ways toward the children we teach in order to become "good" teachers.

THE "GOOD" TEACHER

This section discusses from multiple perspectives what a "good" teacher can be like. Perhaps Barbara's and Pheung's experiences illuminate the question, "How does one become a 'good' teacher?" What questions do teachers need to ask of themselves in order to become "good" teachers?

"The Good Teacher" by Christopher M. Clark (1995) suggests that research on teaching offers three distinct models of good teaching. These are the process-product approach, teacher thinking research, and the teacher knowledge paradigm. Clark asks what teachers themselves say about their best moments and what students remember about their best teachers. The messages from the research communities, practicing teachers, and reflective students are laid side by side and implications for teacher professional development are drawn.

The key points to note in Clark's article are that teachers affect the overall quality of education that tends to limit or enable the next generation of teachers. Good teachers have the following qualities: good knowledge of content, general knowledge of pedagogy, knowledge of curriculum, knowledge of pedagogical content, knowledge of learners and their characteristics, knowledge of educational contexts and educational ends, and knowledge of educational purposes and values. The good teacher is a lifelong learner who performs well in the arena of human relations. According to students, a good teacher is known, encouraged, respected, and led.

They demonstrate ideas so that students will not forget the lessons implicit in the teaching.

What follows are two pieces of writing from the lived experiences of an adult and a child that reflect on the process of teaching and learning. Although many individuals may be able to describe a "good" teacher from whom they have had the benefit of learning, these particular accounts describe an understanding not only of the student but of the needs of the student. In both pieces of writing, the message is clear—good teaching is not only timely but timeless. Here is an article by Moira T. Carley from the 2003 *Globe and Mail*:

Many years ago, during my first year teaching university, after what I though was a fairly engaging lecture, and hoping for some response from the 60 students in front of me I asked them: "What do you think?" An answer I didn't expect came from a long-legged young man sitting in the front row. Continuing to look down at this notebook, he muttered loud enough for me to hear, "Who the hell cares?"

That was when I came to understand that students who sit in class filling their notebooks with my knowledge soon lose interest in learning for themselves. Most survive the drudgery of school by slipping into a state of robotic passivity.

I have since come to realize that most university students commonly spend four years in school working hard for a diploma without ever experiencing the excitement of their own minds at work learning something new. That they can bring their own active intelligence to the learning process is beyond what they can imagine. "Unbelievable!" they say, when they are asked to express their own thoughts and questions in their own words. What they do not know is that the progress or decline of our world—the one we all live in together—depends on our choosing to accept ourselves (or not) as intelligent questioners.

The larger tragedy, as I see it, is that when the spontaneous human desire to question and to understand and to create meaning is not actively engaged in the teaching/learning process, humanity is diminished. The zone of imagination shrinks. Boredom and despair set in. The young inner life ripe for expansion shrivels up for lack of hope. As students learn to play the game of accumulating information without asking their own questions, the curiosity and wonder that five-year-olds bring to school is educated out of them. When I asked my then-20-year-old nephew, once a child totally turned on by curiosity about the world, what he had learned in his first year of university, he said: "I learned how to pass exams."

The fact that computers can do so much for students—even write their papers—offers an exciting opportunity for those of us who want to give back to students the power of learning for themselves. What was once stored in the grooves and chemicals within human brains has become accessible to human fingertips on computer discs. But only when active human intelligence grasps the presence (or absence) of intelligible patterns of meaning does data cease being mere data and a space is created where real personal learning happens.

Given the glut of information available in our time, it is not surprising that students come to school with a hunting-and-gathering attitude toward learning. Teachers can perform, like guides in a museum, pointing to our accumulated knowledge, supervising students' assimilation of other people's knowledge and rewarding them for repeating it on exams. Or we can develop a way to engage students in the experience of their own intelligence at work.

Most teachers and parents would agree with me that the purpose of schooling has been sabotaged when students drift mindlessly from one room to the next at the sound of a bell and are rewarded for accumulating other people's knowledge.

Although I am officially retired from full-time university teaching, for more than 10 years now I have been teaching a course I call The Creative Self. I want my students to learn how to use their own minds creatively by following through on their own questions. The structure of the course is based on the work of Canadian philosopher and theologian Bernard Lonergan (1904–1984), who says the cumulative process of human understanding evolves on a spiral of heightening consciousness. The active learner moves from being attentive to data, to intelligent questioning, to making reasonable judgments based on available evidence, to becoming a responsible maker of value decisions. Students in the course usually come to accept responsibility for their own learning within a teaching/learning framework of collaborative creativity.

One year my course included, for me, a daunting number of football players. I wondered how they would answer the assigned essay question: how Lonergan's explanation of the levels of consciousness could help them understand their own learning process. As well as contributing to my limited football vocabulary, one student, Jeffrey Ross, gave me a description of intelligence that came to him as he was puzzling over the assignment and watching a football game on TV (at the same time!):

> The running back for one team made a spectacular play breaking the tackles of numerous defenders to gallop 25 yards into the end zone. The announcer cried out with great enthusiasm: "What a creative play by the running back!" and that is where it clicked. I asked myself these questions: What about this play was creative? Does something as simple as a 10-second football play have a deeper meaning? As fans and spectators we only see the physical actions of the player, but beneath these actions there is a whole layer of in-depth thought and creativity to make this spectacular action a reality. There is a common football saying that says "run to daylight." The metaphor means that, to a running back, everything that is a dangerous area is dark and shaded because there is normally a defender in that position, but his windows of opportunity normally appear where he can see a crack of daylight shining through the darkness, a weakness in the defense, an area of safety where he can run. He must be very attentive and alert to watch and scan and ask himself when and where this opening will appear and how he will make the passage through. The imagination kicks in and gives him the clue and in this case he did a nifty little spin to get out of the grasp of the defender and successfully hit his daylight hole, and marched into the end zone for the touchdown.

Jeffrey said he was surprised that I wrote "Brilliant!" after this in his essay.

This account reminds us that good teaching depends on knowledge and competence, a willingness to explore new ideas and critically examine traditional knowledge structures, to allow learning to take place in an open and trusting environment, and to respect oneself and one's students but above all to be a caring and supportive individual. The lived experiences of individuals suggest an opportunity to examine not only what has been offered but also what has been missing; to challenge fundamental taken-for-granted assumptions regarding our teaching practices and to challenge inequitable, unjust, or questionable practices.

Letter from Vanessa

Dear Mrs. Hill,

The important thing about you is you hug me wen im sad. Its true that you have a loveley voice. You all ways give us differente senters each day.

And i love you sharing all your gorgus costums in the play house. You taught me and sarah patterns o colers, shaps too.

I had fun lerning my numbers and too share in class. But the important theing about you is you hug me wene im sad.

V n a

P.s. find my puzzle i made for you

This letter was written by a child to her kindergarten teacher. While the letter may have been prompted by the teacher's reading to her class "The Most Important Thing," the child wrote a beautiful letter that is at once revealing and reflective. It is perhaps interesting to note that the child ends her letter with a recognition of her own voice.

IDEAS FOR STUDY

1. In order to think more critically about your own vantage point, write a short vignette as Barbara and Pheung have done that illustrates a lived experience of teaching and/or learning. Write a short reflection on this lived experience. Why is this an important lived experience to you? What does this example say about teaching and learning in schools and society?
2. Use questions asked in Chapter 2 to frame your lived experience. If appropriate, discuss this lived experience in small groups. For convenience, a template has been provided in the Supplementary Material section of this chapter.

3. Develop or introduce an artifact, such as a piece of literature or art, an article, or a creative object that you may use to reflect on qualities of good teaching practice. Discuss with the whole class how these qualities relate to good teaching.
4. How can these qualities be translated into classroom practice for teachers? How can these qualities be translated into classroom practice for teacher educators?

SUPPLEMENTARY MATERIAL: QUESTIONS FOR CRITICAL INQUIRY INTO SCHOOL AND SOCIETY

- Do you think these situations and attitudes still exist in schools? Why?
- Who benefits from it being this way?
- Is this democratic?
- Is there more information you need to help you to understand the situation?
- Is anyone's perspective missing?
- Whose perspective is missing, and why do you think it is missing?
- What does this lived experience not tell you?
- Is there a way to interrupt and rewrite this experience?

REFERENCES

Carley, M. T. 2003. We should try to remain bathed in the divine light of a questioning curiosity. *The Globe and Mail* (Toronto), February 4, A18.

Clark, C. M. 1995. The good teacher. In *Thoughtful Teaching*. New York: Teachers College Press.

Crites, S. 1971. The narrative quality of experience. *Journal of the American Academy of Religion* 39, no. 3: 291–305.

Saint-Exupery, A. de 1943. *The Little Prince*. Trans. K. Woods. New York: Harcourt, Brace & World.

RECOMMENDED READING

Clark, C. M. 1995 The good teacher. In *Thoughtful Teaching*. New York: Teachers College Press.

Part II

STUDENTS' AND TEACHERS' VOICES

Children make the best theorists since they have not yet been educated into accepting our routine social practices as "natural," and so insist on posing to those practices the most embarrassingly general and fundamental questions, regarding them with a wondering estrangement which we adults have long forgotten. Since they do not yet grasp our social practices as inevitable, they do not see why we might not do things differently.

—Terry Eagleton (1990)

There are significant differences between lived experiences and burning issues. Lived experiences may encompass broad or even superficial experiences that have had some impact on teachers' or students' lives. They may be positive or negative in nature. Lived experiences are the sparks which serve to ignite the burning issue. These issues are often less than positive experiences since they help to reveal a deficit in the societal context that, in the interests of critical inquiry, must be addressed. In other words, burning issues are important or pressing issues that arise out of students' lived experiences. They are structured around two themes:

- individual lived experiences and broader cultural frameworks within school and society
- learning from one's own and others' questions for a critical inquiry in order to create a possibility for a pedagogy of hope and school change

Burning issues relate to the purpose of the book through learning to understand one's own lived experience in the context of teacher education and the larger society. In part II, we present excerpts from students' burning issues and discuss relevant issues to consider in courses that focus on critical inquiry.

Students are provided with a framework or rubric for thinking and writing about their burning issues to be shared at the conclusion of the course, as shown in table II.1. This framework includes:

• Background, including reasons for choosing the burning issue in question
• Awareness of broader educational issues
• Connections between lived experience and broader cultural patterns
• Implications for classroom practice

This framework may be presented early in the course so that the preservice students will have time to examine a prior lived experience or a critical incident that arises through their teaching practice. The course continues to evolve as students are asked to think about and risk their own questions which have resulted from interactions with articles, videos, guest speakers, cultural artifacts, poetry and other realia introduced in class. This process of questioning helps focus one burning issue that they choose to explore and share as the culminating activity for hope and school change.

Burning issues written by former preservice students are introduced in this section. The focus is on raising concerns to a conscious level so that students may become aware of the many faces of injustice and suffering and think of ways to interrupt and rewrite these stories. The writing of their own burning issues, then, connects to the third theme of the book, "toward a pedagogy of hope and school change," by asking students to interpret, to consider, and to discuss how they might put their new-found understanding of their lived experience into action in their future classrooms.

Although the curriculum for the course is very carefully planned, one is never really sure what will happen when the students are asked to begin with themselves. Although students are sometimes resistant to look at their own lived experiences, many students became more comfortable addressing difficult questions or issues arising from their own lives as a result of the instructor sharing personal lived experiences.

Table II.1. Burning Issues Rubrics

Categories	Less than B−	B	A−	A	A+
1. Coherence and Structure (10%) —reasons for choice of question (why?) —problem addressed (what?)	not apparent not apparent	present but unclear present but unclear	adequate adequate	clear and coherent clear and coherent	concise and thoughtful concise and thoughtful
2. Awareness of Broader (10%) Educational Issues —awareness of implications	not aware of issues	aware of issues	aware of how issues impact students/teachers/society	deep understanding of how issues impact students/teachers/society	thorough understanding of how issues impact students/teachers/society
3. Application for Classroom (20%) —use of examples/lesson issue	unaware of problem/issue	aware of problem/issue	attempt to address the problem/issue within the classroom	creative attempt to address the problem/issue within the classroom	creative attempt to address the problem/issue within the classroom and beyond
4. Format/Presentation (how?)* (10%)					

*Note: It is expected that all submissions will be presented in an acceptable format, APA (if applicable), in a writing style appropriate to the content, with correct grammar, spelling, and punctuation. Resources are expected to be credible and useful.

BURNING ISSUES: JOHN AND SAM

Here are two excerpts from burning issues that grew out of the lived experiences of one preservice student's disability and another's childhood bereavement. These lived experiences are presented here in order to raise issues that may be pertinent to discussion around implementation of critical inquiry in the preservice classroom and beyond. John's burning issue begins with the following:

> I chose this burning issue because at the age of nineteen I was diagnosed with both Tourette Syndrome and Obsessive-Compulsive Disorder. I do not like to refer to them as disorders. Rather, I prefer to say that I experience symptoms of TS or OCD. Until the time of my diagnosis, I was uncertain of where I was going in life in terms of a career. When the diagnosis came, I quickly changed my major in university to psychology, and began to become interested in the field of education. I educated myself about TS and OCD and . . . began to be a strong advocate for others with special needs. I feel that my diagnosis was somewhat of a calling for me, to help others like me who are struggling with disabilities.

John goes on to give a factual account of the problems associated with these disorders. He speaks of the cultural alienation a child may encounter, and examines how schools have historically segregated these children. His burning issue assignment offers hope, not only by making others aware of Tourette Syndrome and Obsessive-Compulsive Disorder, but also by reframing the issue through offering practical classroom suggestions for supporting children with these problems. John has, in effect, interrupted a cultural pattern of exclusion that often causes children to feel a strong sense of alienation. In his own practicum, he read a children's book entitled *Hi, I'm Adam*, which he offered as one strategy for helping teachers and children understand what it is like for a child to live with Tourette Syndrome. John's burning issue serves as an opportunity for students to understand how their local experiences can be viewed as a universal condition.

John was a preservice student who was able to immediately address and share his burning issue. Others shared lived experiences elicited from their practicums. However, not all students were grateful for the opportunity to explore and question. Sam's burning issue is set in counterpoint to John's.

Sam initially reported not being comfortable with sharing personal lived experiences and asked to do a "traditional" research paper instead. Sam was reminded that he did not have to start with his own lived experience, but could use the practicum experience as a springboard for the burning issue assignment. Sam decided to use his own lived experience and handed in his assignment well before the due date. Included is an excerpt from Sam's burning issue:

> How can we, as trusted and caring educators, assist bereaved children in dealing with grief, in order to assist the child in the painful process of mourning in the near term, and embrace their emotional well being in the long term?
>
> When I was eight years old, my six-year-old sister drowned in a public pool during the summer holiday. Our family structure, which until that moment was very stable, was shaken. I lost my kid sister, and consequently lost the foster brother I also had at the time, since my parents were physically and emotionally unable to continue as foster parents. I truly was alone in what previously was a house alive with children. My parents gave me all the love they could, but my mother was crippled by the grief and unable to assist me with my own grieving. My father, a very stoic man, was also unable to help me, since he was not equipped with the emotional skills to deal with his own grief issues, never mind my own.

The key points that Sam makes in his burning issue are that children can experience bereavement as a result of a death, through a family separation, or by moving to another country. They experience immediate and intermediate symptoms. The most appropriate teacher response is to act immediately, since ignoring this issue often results in additional problems. Effective strategies include listening to the student, communicating with parents, and clarifying the conditions surrounding the loss. An effective teacher can help the student work through the loss by creating a safe classroom environment, by discussing the stages of grief, through the creation of memory books, or by reading stories on similar themes. Further assistance could include helping to build a more healthy attitude toward death by developing science units on life cycles or by inviting experts on the subject in to talk with students.

Through this lived experience, Sam reminds us that the death of a child is not a natural occurrence and, when it happens, families can be shaken apart. In his paper, he also elaborates on how this unnatural occurrence is compounded by the preoccupation of Western society with the sanitization of death. Yet perhaps the saddest part in all of this is that Sam's burning issue reveals that children are often left to walk the road of grief alone. Historically, children have often been seen as not having feelings and emotions of the same magnitude as adults. Cultural patterns are revealed through Sam's writing.

Sam's courage is impressive in confronting a tragedy that affects him to this day. However, completing this assignment helped him work through his personal issues so that, rather than hiding behind his own personal grief, he now feels more confident in being able to help children who are grappling with the same pain.

These excerpts are but two examples of the many burning issues that have surfaced over the years. Others focus on equity, diversity, and difference and will be examined in more depth in this section through a layering of cultural artifacts such as theoretical articles, newspaper editorials, and other realia. By beginning locally, with themselves and their own lived experiences, through sharing and experiencing the multiplicity of perspectives within their preservice classes, these students took up the opportunity to extend their understanding beyond the individual to the universal, to become citizens of the world (Freire 1998).

The next part of this text, Students' and Teachers' Voices, presents situations in which lived experiences are at issue. Because burning issues identify significant issues of importance for individuals, connecting the personal life experiences to the broader problematics in society, these issues assist in deconstructing teacher identity around issues such as bullying, homophobia and diverse sexual orientation, sexism and feminist issues in teaching, diversity and social stratification, and anti-discrimination education.

Each of these issues can inform inclusive teaching, learning, and classroom practices since each lived experience tends to transcend the margins that define it. Each issue may be examined through multiple lenses that may at once focus on gender, class, and moral issues, to mention only a sampling of possibilities.

The construction of burning issues, with effective layering of complexity and context, is important in meeting the needs of both preservice and inservice teachers. This section, from chapter 4 through chapter 8, represents a collection of some of the more typical burning issues that have arisen from students' lived experiences. Chapter 4 discusses bullying in the elementary school. Chapter 5 discusses homophobia and diverse sexual orientation, and chapter 6 focuses on feminist issues in teaching through a discussion of the components of issues surrounding inequity. Chapter 7 inquires into issues common to diversity and social stratification. Chapter 8 discusses anti-discrimination education. These burning issues may be useful in developing a critique that students, teachers, and their inclusive community may require in order to understand the process of becoming more critical in their thinking.

While it is true that these and similar issues recur from time to time, each issue represents a process that points to the critiquing and thinking through of questions that the students themselves have raised after reading these burning issues. In addition, students had access to theoretical and research articles that served to supplement and complement their own issues. These articles are summarized in each chapter.

REFERENCES

Eagleton, T. (1990). *The Significance of Theory*. Cambridge: Blackwell.
Freire, P. (1998). *Pedagogy of the Heart*. New York: Continuum.

Chapter Four

Bullying in the Elementary School

"His real name's Piggy!"
"Piggy, Piggy! Oh, Piggy!"
    A storm of laughter arose and even the tiniest child joined in. For the moment, the boys were a closed circuit of sympathy with Piggy outside . . .

— William Golding (1965)

Bullying has probably been a part of human life since mankind first crawled out of the primordial ooze. Since the dawn of time, power differentials have been institutionalized through various forms of bullying in school playgrounds and in school staff rooms and extend beyond the walls of the educational facility to the greater community itself. In fact, bullying is a worldwide phenomenon (Olweus 1993; Whitney and Smith 1993). The two most common bullying venues are the school playground and the classroom (Borg 1999; Whitney and Smith 1993), followed by "on the way home," the school corridor, and "on the way to school" (Borg 1999). The fact that the two most common venues for bullying are areas where the teachers have responsibilities for supervision has important implications for effective intervention.

But what is bullying and why is it such an issue? Bullying is a form of violence in which one or more perpetrators inflict physical or psychological harm in order to gain power over one or more victims (Bickmore 2000). Bullying occurs when a student is exposed, repeatedly and over time, to negative actions on the part of one or more students (Olweus 1996). "Negative actions" refer to physical contact such as punching, hitting, kicking pushing, shoving, pinching, restraining, or tripping as well as verbal abuse such as teasing, name-calling, insults, sarcastic remarks, racist or sexist comments, gossip, threats, or intimidation. Negative actions also include making faces, glaring, threatening gestures, and ignoring or intentional exclusion from a group (Temrick 2000). While not all aggressive behaviour can be considered bullying as it is not necessarily repeated over a period of time (Olweus 1996), bullying is a response to various kinds of conflict:

- Intrapersonal conflict (inside a person)
- Interpersonal conflict (between two or more people)
- Social conflict (between two or more social groups or between a group and a larger social system)

Harassment is a form of bullying that uses social inequality to gain power over its victims. While sexual harassment takes advantage of sexism and homophobia to target females and some males, ethnocentric harassment takes advantage of racism to target people from minority groups. Social exclusion is another form of bullying that inflicts harm by isolating individuals or denying them the opportunity to be valued members of a social group. All bullying serves (consciously or unconsciously) the intent by those who are more powerful to intimidate, control, or deny human rights to those less powerful (Bickmore 2000). Bullying presents a conflict that underlies its most obvious symptoms. What follows is Myriam's, a student teacher's, burning issue: bullying.

Bullying: A Student Teacher's Perspective

Bullying is finally being recognized as a serious problem by the media, by schools, and by parents. While this is a major step, everyone involved with children needs to develop a strong sense of urgency [about this issue] so that students can grow up without being physically and mentally tortured by other children. The lives of students who are being bullied are an everyday living hell. The bullies suffer, too, in the long run, because they often fail to develop empathy with others.

The point of this paper is to explore how we can move forward toward taking swift measures to end the fact that for many children life is a "war zone" (Honey 2002) due to bullying. My suggestion is that teachers can take *direct and meaningful* action by infusing all subjects they teach with conflict-resolution theory. I realize that to end bullying we need to take various actions from many different areas; however, I believe that by teaching conflict-resolution theory, we, as teachers, can instill a mindset that will go a long way to helping children cope with bullies.

The Issue

It is only in the last few years that the issue of "bullying" has received attention; before that the parents or teachers of a bully simply said "Oh, ignore it and it will go away," "It is just a phase that children go through," and all the other platitudes that concealed an ominous problem.

Bullying is a menacing predicament that can end in the death of a child! Research reveals that approximately 20 percent of all pupils are implicated, either as a victim or a bully (Peplar, Craig, Zeigler, and Charach 1993). Bullying in schools arises as early as kindergarten and persists into postsecondary school.

Bullying in some situations leads to disastrous consequences, such as suicide or murder (Olweus 1993). It can often cause pupils permanent psychological wounds; victims often suffer loneliness and low self-worth, which can continue into later life. The learning ability of a victim suffers because of difficulty concentrating on schoolwork (*Globe and Mail*, March 23, 2002. Focus F9: Overview of Roy Baumeister's paper, titled "Effects of Social Exclusion on Cognitive Processes: Anticipates Aloneness Reduces Intelligent Thought," scheduled to be published in the *Journal of Personality and Social Psychology* in the fall). Children who are allowed to bully have a greater likelihood of being involved in other types of crimes, and as adults, to encounter marital and spousal troubles, to have hostile children, and to suffer work-related problems. Additionally, other children who do not give aid to the victim often suffer from guilt and they perceive that they, too, are not in a secure environment (Craig and Peplar 1999).

Personal Issue

Bullying is a burning issue for me for four reasons:

First, as a child in elementary and secondary school, I witnessed numerous children being bullied unmercifully. Although I knew that the bully was being cruel, I never intervened to help the victim; I waited until the bully left before I consoled the hurt child. I continually felt guilty that I was a bystander to vile behaviour. On reflection, I realize I was afraid to challenge the bully in case he/she turned on me. In essence, the bully's power was so overarching that it prevented me, when younger, from acting in a sympathetic fashion; the bully made me an indirect accomplice.

Second, bullying is a burning issue for me because some years ago, a friend invited me to listen to a speech on "Forgiveness"—this talk was delivered by The Reverend David Lang (father of Jason Lang, a gifted 17-year-old [who was] shot in Taber, Alberta, when two bullies burst into his school). During Rev. Lang's speech, I was horrified that he, or anyone, could lose his son so needlessly. This was a riveting moment because a newspaper account suddenly came to life before my eyes: here was a real person standing before me who had needlessly lost a loved and cherished son.

Third, bullying is a burning issue for me because in the last few weeks, during the criminal hearing regarding the suicide of Dawn-Marie Wesley, the 14-year-old from Abbotsford who committed suicide because of bullying, I was shocked to discover the details of her situation. Moreover, when I discussed the case with my neighbour, who is a pediatrician (Dr. P.), she told me that every week she deals with children who are having physical and emotional problems because of bullying. Indeed, she recounted that last July she was called to an exclusive summer camp, north of Toronto, to attend to a 12-year-old child who had unsuccessfully attempted suicide as a result of emotional bullying. The situation was hushed [up] because neither the camp owners nor the parents wanted publicity. The two 13-year-old girls who did the bullying were allowed to complete their stay at camp; meanwhile, the victim was hospitalized for treatment.

While Dr. P. was outraged at the situation, the victim's parents insisted on confidentiality. Under the circumstances, Dr. P.'s follow-up on the case was very limited. She also shared with me that many patients in her practice suffer the daily torments of bullying and they often consider suicide as a way to end their suffering. Dr. P. described the lives of children who are miserable simply because other children pick on them. Almost all the bullying is of a psychological nature and usually involves exclusion and whispering rumours.

Last, bullying is a burning issue for me because in my first and second practicum I saw children being bullied in both subtle and obvious ways. While I intervened as often as I thought was needed, I realized that, despite our awareness, schools and society are not effectively tackling this dismal and insidious problem. Although schools have anti-bullying initiatives in place, the reality is that numerous children continue to suffer anxiety and terror daily at the hands of other children.

I propose that bullying is such an appalling problem that it should be considered a national emergency, much like the efforts that governments and other institutions undertake [to] combat international terrorism. Bullying is terrorism—it is a group of our children inflicting major physical and psychological damage on another.

Anti-Bullying Initiatives in Schools

Virtually all schools have introduced anti-bullying initiatives; however, the problem continues at a shocking rate. Many resources are dedicated to preventing violence in schools, but bullying still persists every day. Many teachers are ill equipped to deal with anti-social behaviour like bullying simply because they have not been trained to do so and because teaching is so demanding (*Globe and Mail*, March 27, 2002, A7. Ms. Reggi Balabanov, President of the B. C. Confederation of Parent Advisory Councils).

According to various parents' groups, progress is being made in schools to eliminate bullying, but by and large, it continues. The president of the B.C. Confederation of Parent Advisory Councils states that greater action must be implemented. Schools must be actively involved in eliminating bullying. Anti-bullying initiatives should consist of something more than just awareness of the topic—it must include *action*: "Those binders need to be opened and there needs to be training to give staff the capacity to deal with those issues" (*Globe and Mail*, March 27, 2002, A7. Ms. Reggi Balabanov, President of the B. C. Confederation of Parent Advisory Councils).

Conflict Management and the Curriculum:
One Method to Help End Bullying

Since it is impossible for children to coexist without some conflict, they should be taught conflict-resolution theory as early as kindergarten. It is never too early to teach children how to handle conflict and harassment. Bullying in schools often begins from the first day of school (interview with Prof. Wendy Craig, CBC—March 26, 2002). The bullying frequently starts over something as inconsequential as a spat and then snowballs into a hellish situation where other children abandon the victim for fear of invoking the bully's wrath. Jennifer Connolly of York University's LaMarsh Centre for Research into Violence and Conflict Resolution notes that students are often picked on for having supposedly "minor differences," for example, a lisp, wearing glasses, or having freckles or for being "too fat," "too thin," too tall, too small, and so forth (Honey 2002).

Conflict-resolution theory can be helpful to children in understanding and minimizing the difficulties caused by bullying. During all curriculum subjects, where possible, the topic of conflict resolution should be integrated.

For instance, language arts class offers a wonderful opportunity to discuss conflicts contained in a story or a novel. By infusing teaching with this approach, students will develop skills in reasoning and critical thinking. In a novel, for instance, by identifying the main ideas in each chapter, the pupils will learn to describe the story's elements and make inferences regarding the characters and action; they then can discuss similar situations in their own lives.

By articulating the conflict in a story and how it might be resolved, the children will learn to make predictions while reading; additionally, they will understand how to handle parallel circumstances in their own lives. They will conclude that conflict is natural and that it can be resolved without bullying.

In drama class, for example, through role-playing the problem scenarios in a text, the pupils will learn to retell a story and adapt it for presentation in a dramatic format. In doing this, they will perceive how a conflict can escalate or how it can be diffused. Pupils may discuss their own related story where they may have been a victim, aggressor, or a bystander (Sheanh 1996).

As teachers, we must go beyond policing pupils in the schoolyard; we must help children internalize the values of conflict-resolution theory so that our work will have [a] lasting impact. As Gary Sheanh states in his book, "In conflict resolution, as with life, everything is connected" (96).

Suggestion for an Integrated Unit

In a recent language arts lesson in my last practicum, I integrated conflict-resolution theory into the reading of a novel with my Grade 3 students. Appendix 1 (below) gives an example of how the novel allowed me to teach an anti-bullying message while meeting the curriculum requirements for language arts.

Internet Sources of Help

Teachers might consider posting this Web site right in the classroom so that if a child feels incapable of reaching [out to] a teacher or parent for help, he or she may get it on the Internet: www.bullying.org. This Web site is considered to be the world's biggest bullying-related Web site. It contains opportunities for children to get advice on bullying, and it allows them to tell their stories. They can also submit their drawings depicting their situation. The Web site is run by Bill Belsey, a teacher who taught in Nunavut for twenty years. He set up the site in 1999 after the killing of Jason Lang during school by two bullies.

Appendix 1

Novel: Judy Blume, *Tales of a Fourth Grade Nothing* (New York: Bantam, 1991).

Summary of the Story

Peter Hatcher lives in New York City with his mother, father, and two-year-old brother, Fudge, in an old apartment building. Peter often becomes upset with the behaviour of his younger brother Fudge. He is frequently embarrassed and ashamed of the scenes Fudge creates.

Peter feels that his parents allow Fudge to get away with many things and he feels that they give him too much attention. He is very discouraged with his situation and often feels like a "fourth grade nothing." When Fudge walks off with Dribble, Peter's pet turtle, it is the last straw for Peter.

The story also covers Peter's relationships with his school friends, particularly Jimmy and Sheila, the other children living in his apartment building, and those in the neighbourhood. Much of the time, his relationship with Sheila is unsatisfactory because Peter believes she is "bossy" and a "know-it-all."

Purpose/Context

This story is appropriate for a Grade 3–level reader because the main character, Peter, is roughly the same age as children in that grade. The novel is set in an inner-city neighbourhood in New York City; the characters come from diverse cultures. The novelist addresses gender issues when she outlines some of the difficulties that occur when boys and girls play together. Additionally, the novel discusses the problems that children experience when they live in a cramped environment. Finally, there are many situations in the book where the main character must make accommodations to children who come from diverse backgrounds.

Grade 3 students will enjoy reading this novel, and it will give them the opportunity to discuss causes of conflict and develop ideas on how to manage it.

Learning Expectations

By reading and discussing the text, students will develop skills in reasoning and critical thinking. By identifying the main ideas in each chapter, the pupils will learn to describe the story's elements and make inferences regarding the characters and action. By articulating the conflict in the story and how it might be resolved, the children will learn to make predictions while reading. Additionally, by debating the various upsets that occur, the students will understand how to make judgments about the book's contents. Finally, through role-playing the quarrels in the tale, the pupils will learn to retell a story and adapt it for presentation in a dramatic format.

Rationale

I chose this novel because it does an excellent job of bringing to the forefront the issues that cause conflict for children in their interactions with parents, siblings, friends, and classmates.

Another student, Linda, stated that the spectacle of seeing her brother bullied on a regular basis, an experience that eventually resulted in her brother dropping out of school, motivated her to become a teacher in order to ensure that no child endures the pain and humiliation her brother faced. She is committed to stopping bullying and creating a safe school environment where children are encouraged, respected, recognized, and rewarded for their individual worth. She says that every child deserves to achieve success and that it is our responsibility as educators to ensure that this occurs.

It may be helpful to gain further insight into this issue through a parent's lived experience of having to deal with many of the complexities of the real world of bullying in schools as interpreted by a child:

Bullying: A Parent's Perspective

Because I had spoken to my son several times about breaking school rules, I was exasperated. What I say to my young son is not all I want to tell him, but I try not to overcomplicate things. I think of the inadequacy and shortfalls of the judicial system in our country and know the impossibility of justice in a schoolyard.

What I know for sure is that I don't want my child to hurt anyone. I say, "Hitting is wrong. It doesn't matter how annoying someone is, hitting is wrong. Doesn't matter if he hit you first, you shouldn't fight back."

My son's regular bus driver wasn't driving; the substitute didn't know the route and got lost several times. The bus trip was double its normal time. I doubt the fight would have happened if the bus driver who knows the group, the route, and is good at preventing fights had been driving.

I think to myself; this is how lives are changed; how the course of many a trial is influenced by happenstance and how many outcomes would be altered with minor changes.

Another incident my son was involved in [during] this same week occurred when the snow fort he and his friend were building was attacked. He got mad and retaliated against the other fort. I asked him what his friends did when the opponents were attacking. He told me they just went right on building. I tell him that's what he should have done. He says, "That's stupid, then they'll just wreck your fort."

I listen to my children and their friends talk in my house. They have a good sense of what is right and what is wrong. They also understand that there is a gulf between what actually happens and how it all pans out. You're lucky if you have lots of friends because they will be your witnesses. One boy describes the outcome of one situation as being resolved unfairly because someone "pulled a lie" for someone else.

I am amazed by the intricacy of the underground politics of schoolyard justice. My son says there's lots of hitting; you only get in trouble when someone tells on you. He doesn't ever tell on anyone; he thinks that's wrong.

I tell him not to hit back but to move away, and he tells me in an exasperated voice, "No, then they'll just think they can hit me."

I told my son that he will get a bad reputation if he hits people and gets suspended, but he tells me that kids who get suspended actually have sort of a good reputation, a tough reputation, and people don't bother them. My older son told me the same thing a few years ago. I tell my son he won't be popular if he hits people and he says it doesn't really matter:

The kids who are popular are the ones who are good in sports.

What I want to say is that the world is terribly unfair. I want to tell him to stay out of trouble as much as possible and not to get involved in fights. I want to tell him that fights can go horribly wrong. But I tell my children if someone is beating up someone else they must step in. They tell me that they'll get beaten up instead. "Run and get a teacher," I say, and they agree that this is a solution, but they are frightened of being labeled a tattletale.

I worry about the amount of time spent in school meting out punishments in a system with unreliable child witnesses, parents as lawyers, and principals as judges—principals who have a myriad of other responsibilities and duties. I shake my head and wonder how it ever got like this.

I keep going over what I can say to my son about not fighting. I want to say something that he will understand, something that makes sense.

I am lying awake the night he is sent home from school, unable to sleep, the weight of my child's transgressions enfolding me. Then I remember something an eager young lifeguard said when my eldest daughter was taking lessons at the local outdoor pool many years ago. When my young son started running around the pool the lifeguard called out "WALK" and my son began to walk. The lifeguard turned to me and said, "We try not to say 'don't run' they never listen to that."

The next morning, I asked my son what kind of person he admires and who he wants to be like. I tell him to be the kind of person he wants to be. Be kind. Be a leader. Be the type of person that other kids want to spend time with. It's hard to explain the look on my son's face, but I could see that he was listening, so I stopped. But then, to cover all the bases, I did add, "And of course, don't hurt anyone and keep your hands to yourself." [The author of this first-person perspective, Kathryn Davies, lives in Newmarket, Ontario.]

In a paper prepared for an anti-bullying project, Kathy Bickmore (2000) suggests that conflict resolution can assist in understanding and alleviating bullying. Her paper highlights three dimensions of conflict resolution:

- Establishing procedures
- Developing knowledge and skills for handling conflict
- Nurturing relationships in the school community

The establishment of procedures ranges from negative peacekeeping to positive peacemaking. Development of knowledge and skills among teachers, students, and others connected to the school is essential to prevent an escalation of problems related to bullying. Nurturing relationships in the school community that are resilient for handling conflict operate through reducing competition and inequity and increase flexibility and openness to change.

All three of these elements are essential for preventing and resolving bullying conflicts because these dimensions of conflict resolution involve learning. Simply put, knowledge is essential for action and people learn by observing and following models of conflict management in context.

BULLIES AND THEIR VICTIMS

Typical bullies have a desire for power and dominance. Also, bullies are often surrounded by silent bullies or "passive observers" who provide support and approval for the bully that provides the bully with status and encourages continuation of the bullying behaviour (Olweus 1996; Temrick 2000). Boys are most often both the perpetrators and the victims of bullying (Borg 1999; Froschl and Sprung 1999; Olweus 1996). Victims often appear physically weaker than their counterparts, and this may make them more vulnerable to attack (Ballard et al. 1999; Olweus 1996, 1993). Contrary to popular belief, other physical characteristics such as height, weight, eyesight, or clothing that are considered unusual are not factors that seem to lead to victimization (Olweus 1996, 1993). Because victims fear going to school, their apprehension limits their ability to concentrate and may lead to marginal or poor academic results. Feeling constantly anxious and insecure, it is little wonder that victims' absenteeism and dropout rates are higher than those of their peers (Connell and Farrington 1996).

THE CONSEQUENCES OF BULLYING

Not only can bullying create a negative and disruptive atmosphere in the classroom and playground, it may also interfere with students' ability to learn and teachers' ability to teach. The effects of bullying at school spill over into the lives of both the victims and the perpetrators as well as those of their families. Suicide and violent retaliation causing injury or death are two extreme responses of victims of bullying. Other responses may include habit disorders, behaviour extremes, overly adaptive behaviours, and developmental lags (Neese 1989). Furthermore, as adults, victims may be subject to depression and isolation and may suffer from poorer self-esteem than their nonvictimized peers (Olweus 1996, 1993).

Bullies also seem to be at increased risk for running into difficulties later in life. By the time they reach high school, bullies seem to be less popular and have fewer friends (Olweus 1996). They are also more likely to run into problems with the law. Bullies often retain their aggressive behaviour well into their adult years, and this reduces their ability to form, develop, and maintain meaningful relationships. As adults, bullies tend to suffer from higher rates of substance abuse, domestic violence, and other violent crimes (Olweus 1996).

DEALING WITH BULLYING

But how does a child on a school playground effectively prevent an episode of bullying? Either as a victim or as a spectator there needs to be some form of easily accessible mediation. It may not be enough to run for the nearest adult because the playground supervisor may not be immediately present. Intervention in an act of bullying takes some intestinal fortitude, but Bickmore's (2000) dimensions of conflict resolution may still be appropriate. Establishment of procedures may be interpreted as early intervention. A commanding "Stop!" is often sufficient to catch the bully off guard and change the focus of the aggression. This can be immediately followed up by a direction as interpreted by the development of knowledge and skills for handling conflict. This direction can be "I don't want you to . . ." followed by a more nurturing comment aimed at causing a certain amount of self-awareness and developing a positive climate for reflection (nurturing relationships in the school community). Something as simple as "How would you like it if somebody did this to you?" may be quite effective in resolving or at least reducing the impact of bullying on a specific occasion.

Needless to say, this will ultimately have little impact unless there is a wider effort on the part of the larger school community, in the classrooms and beyond, to deal with the underlying issues attendant in bullying, the obvious and overt part of which is only a symptom of other underlying issues. Teachers may take the opportunity to incorporate anti-bullying strategies into the curriculum as part of a comprehensive anti-bullying program. Some of these strategies may include increasing awareness and knowledge about bullying through dispelling myths about such behaviour. These myths include that bullying is a normal part of growing up, that bullying will toughen a victim up, or that bullies are simply putting up a tough front to mask their real feelings. Staff, students, teachers, and parents may wish to be educated about the long-term effects of bullying.

By enlisting active involvement and support on the part of teachers and parents, adults may come to realize how crucial it is to provide sufficient adult supervision at appropriate times during the schoolday. Teachers may also be expected to intervene in any situation where they see bullying behaviour and deliver the unequivocal message to bullies and their victims and to their parents that bullying is neither accepted nor tolerated.

Developing clear rules against bullying behaviour in concert with students will help the classroom rules gain greater importance for the students. When students help to develop rules, they are much more likely to respect and follow them. Creating such rules together presents an opportunity for the class to discuss bullying behaviour. Students may come forth with examples of bullying behaviour and discussion may revolve around ways to minimize or eliminate such anti-social practices.

Providing support and protection for the victims will allow the victims to know that they are valued and respected individuals. Also, discussing social skills with individuals or with the class, as opportunity or necessity dictates, may help both bullies and victims overcome underlying issues. The school, in any case, may ensure that any intervention on the part of the school or the staff does not result in the acceleration of the issues at hand.

Teaching conflict-resolution skills to the entire school may help students and teachers learn to identify feelings and actively listen to others. Students may benefit from learning problem-solving skills and strategies. In addition, both staff and students may benefit from learning to cooperate, respect, and sympathize with one another. The study of literature is often an excellent way for students to learn about conflict, as every book has some form of conflict in it. Teaching students to recognize and deal with problem situations in literature can help them effectively solve problems in everyday life. Role-playing is also an effective tool for learning about bullying as students gain opportunities to experience firsthand the power imbalance present in bullying situations. Also, creating a safe classroom environment is one of the most important things that a teacher can do in order to address problems of bullying. The teacher, in this way, is able to let students know that they are respected, that the teacher is committed to their success and happiness, and that the teacher is available to help them whenever assistance is required.

IMPLICATIONS FOR CLASSROOM PRACTICE

Elementary teachers play a very important role in the lives of their students. Teachers and the students' parents are directly responsible for helping students develop into well-adjusted and productive members of society. Teachers' attitudes and responses to bullying play a defining role in determining the extent of bullying in a school or classroom. Failure to intervene may be caused by any number of factors, including not being aware of the incident, wanting students to work out their difficulties themselves, wanting to discourage tattling, or even thinking that bullying is a natural part of growing up (Froschl and Sprung 1999). However, when teachers do not intervene, a powerful message is sent to the students, who see the teachers' lack of response to bullying as condoning the behaviour.

Teachers want every student to feel welcome and safe at school. Research has shown that bullying is a serious impediment to these goals and to student goals in later life. It is imperative that teachers learn about such issues as bullying since misconceptions abound regarding bullying behaviour and its implications. Teachers' attitudes about bullying play a crucial role in determining the extent to which bullying occurs at school. Implementation of a successful intervention program will depend on careful planning and cooperation among students, teachers, and parents. As a result of these efforts, students, bullies, and victims alike will have greater opportunities to develop both academically and personally.

It is particularly challenging to reduce school-based bullying because this kind of conflict involves unequal power relations among students, which in turn are influenced by the complex social contexts of communities and schools. There are many different approaches to conflict-resolution education, most with good potential to facilitate the knowledge and skill dimension of conflict resolution. However, without attention to procedural and relationship dimensions of conflict resolution, as well as to skills, even this broad array of approaches will be insufficient to prevent or resolve power-based conflicts such as bullying (Bickmore 2000). As educators become more conscious of learning opportunities pertaining to conflict resolution that already exist in schools, they can begin to foster even more effective anti-bullying contexts.

CONCLUSIONS

Bullying is the assertion of power through aggression that provides the perpetrator with a means of gaining status, power, and control. Bullying behaviour does not simply disappear of its own volition but often evolves into criminal activity, including sexual harassment, domestic violence, gang activity, and criminal assault (Craig and Peplar 1999). For both the victim and the bully, consequences of exposure to violence, symbolic or real, may be dire. Recent medical research indicates that exposure to ongoing abuse and violence can permanently alter the young student's neurological activity. This damaging of the brain can create anti-social behaviour that may be impossible to change (Teicher 2002).

Thus, for practical, aesthetic, and social reasons, among many others, bullying is a serious issue that requires attention within and outside any and all institutions of education. The power differentials that lie at the heart of bullying are often an appropriate place to begin a critical inquiry into this phenomenon. It is this power differential that robs the victim of a voice, self-respect, and the respect of others and a subsequent loss of self-esteem. This is a tremendous loss of human potential that engenders exponentially accelerating loss for the society at large. Bullying can be seen as an issue of social justice that has the potential to affect all of society in negative ways, from increased medical assistance to demands for incarceration as bullies, and occasionally their victims, move toward adulthood, perhaps finding themselves either at odds with the law or attempting to fix broken lives in retrospect. The cost in the lack of development of human potential is also significant and is in fact immeasurable, for we can never know how life would be for all of us if bullying were nonexistent. As a measure of equity, equality, and individual rights, bullying must be seen as preventable and worthy of preventing. Steps can be taken by schools, individuals, families, and friends to ensure that bullying issues are dealt with as summarily as possible through moving toward a preventative model. It is in this way that democracy within our schools can be promoted and may help to foster a brighter future not just for the victims of bullying but for us all. It is important to be vigilant, conscious of the issues, and knowledgeable about the remedies and to continue to inquire critically into the nature, the causes, the effects, and the resources available to prevent this type of social justice issue from continuing to cause harm and unnecessary suffering among the citizens of tomorrow.

IDEAS FOR STUDY

1. Describe an event in your life that shows that you have been a bully, a victim of bullying, or an observer of an instance where someone was bullied. What were the dynamics at play in this instance?
2. Discuss the above instance in small groups. Are the dynamics that you have chosen similar to the dynamics of other instances? Do these dynamics appear to be universal?
3. Discuss these dynamics in large groups. What role does a bully play in such an instance? What role does the victim play? What about the observer? What steps can each of these individuals take to overcome bullying? Discuss these in the large group.
4. How can institutions deal with issues of bullying? Prepare a code of ethics on the topic of bullying. Discuss in small groups and then in large groups. Combine and decide on a final draft of a useful code of ethics for your future use.
5. What role can parents play in helping to prevent bullying? In small groups, decide how you would encourage parents to take an active role in the eradication and prevention of bullying. Write this up in a form that would be useful to the individual teacher or to the educational institution. Discuss your write-ups with the large group for the purpose of using these various methods in a concerted effort to reduce bullying in schools.
6. Ask students to find teacher resources or journal articles about bullying. Give each student ten minutes from each class to present in groups of four or five.

REFERENCES

Ballard, M., et al. 1999. Bullying and school violence: A proposed prevention program. *NASSP Bulletin* 6, no. 7 (May): 38–47.

Bickmore, K. 2000. The role of conflict resolution education in overcoming bullying. Paper prepared for the Japan-Canada Anti-Bullying Project Final Report.

Borg, M. G. 1999. The extent and nature of bullying among primary and secondary schoolchildren. *Educational Research* 41, no. 2 (Summer): 137–153.

Connell, A., and D. Farrington. 1996. Bullying among incarcerated young offenders: Developing an interview schedule and some preliminary results. *Journal of Adolescence* 19, no. 1 (February): 75–88.

Craig, W., and D. Peplar. 1999. Children who bully: Will they just grow out of it? *Orbit: A Commentary on the World of Education* 29, no. 4: 16–19.

Froschl, M., and B. Sprung. 1999. On purpose: Addressing teasing and bullying in early childhood. *Young Children* 54, no. 2 (March): 70–72.

Golding, W. 1965. *Lord of the Flies*. Harmondsworth, England: Penguin.

Honey, Kim. 2002. Everyday war zone. *Globe & Mail*, March 30, F1.

Neese, L. A. 1989. Psychological maltreatment in schools: Emerging issues for counselors. *Elementary School Guidance and Counseling* 23: 193–199.

Olweus, D. 1996. Bully/victim problems in school. *Prospects* 26, no. 2 (June): 331–359.

Olweus, D. 1993. *Bullying at School: What We Know and What We Can Do*. Cambridge, Mass.: Blackwell.*Canadian Journal of Community Mental Health.*

Peplar, D., W. Craig, S. Zeigler, and A. Charach. 1993. An evaluation of an anti-bullying intervention in Toronto schools. *Canadian Journal of Community Mental Health.*

Sheanh, G. 1996. *Helping Kids Deal with Conflict: An Everyday Resource for All Teachers and Parents*. Winnipeg, Man.: Peguis Publishers.

Teicher, M. H. 2002. Scars that won't heal: The neurobiology of child abuse. *Scientific American* (March): 68–83.

Temrick, P. 2000. Say no to bullying. Presented at the employment preparation conference for pre-service teacher candidates in Toronto, Ontario, December.

Whitney, I., and P. K. Smith. 1993. A survey of the nature and extent of bullying in junior/middle and secondary schools. *Educational Research* 3, no. 5: 3–25.

RECOMMENDED READING

Picture Books

Angelou, M., and J.-M. Basquiat. 1993. *Life Doesn't Frighten Me at All*. New York: Stewart, Tabori and Chang.

Browne, A. 1985. *Willy the Champ*. New York: Alfred A. Knopf.

Cannon, J. 2000. *Crickwing*. San Diego, Calif.: Harcourt Brace.

Nickle, J. 1999. *The Ant Bully*. New York: Scholastic Inc.

Stones, R. 1993. *Don't Pick on Me: How to Handle Bullying*. Markham, Ont.: Pembroke Publishers.

Novels

Bloor, E. 1997. *Tangerine*. New York: Scholastic Inc.

Conly, J. L. 1998. *While No One Was Watching*. New York: HarperCollins.

Flake, S. 2001. *The Skin I'm In*. New York: Corgi Books.

Golding, W. 1995. *Lord of the Flies*. New York: Faber & Faber.

Hogg, G. 1998. *Scrambled Eggs and Spider Legs*. New York: HarperCollins.

Paterson, K. 2001. *The Field of Dogs*. New York: HarperCollins.

Videos

Elkind, D. 1996. *Groark Learns About Bullying*. San Francisco, Calif.: Live Wire Media. VHS videocassette, 27 min.

Vanderslice, C. 1996. *How I Learned Not to Be Bullied*. Pleasantville, N.Y.: Sunburst Communications. VHS videocassette, 15 min., teacher's guide.

Scripts

Brooks, M., and M. Hunter. 1995. *I Met a Bully on the Hill*. Toronto: Playwrights Union of Canada.

Foon, D. *Seesaw*. Toronto: Playwrights Union of Canada.

Professional Reading

Batsche, G. M., and H. M. Knoff. 1994. Bullies and their victims: Understanding a pervasive problem in the schools. *School Psychology Review* 23, no. 2: 165–174.

Clabough, K. G. 1998. School bullies. *Educational Horizons* 76, no. 4: 163–165.

Craig, W., and D. Peplar. 1999. Children who bully: Will they just grow out of it? *Orbit* 29, no. 4: 16–19.

Gibbs, J. 2000. Tribes: A new way of learning and being together. Sausalito, Calif.: CenterSource Systems.

Hahn, C. A. 1997. *Growing in Authority: Relinquishing Control*. Toronto: Doubleday.

Horsman, J. 1999. *Too Scared to Learn*. Toronto: McGilligan Books.

Johnson, D., and R. Johnson. 1996. Conflict resolution and peer mediation programs in elementary and secondary schools. *Review of Educational Research*
   66, no. 4 (Winter): 459–506.

Rigby, K. 1998. *Bullying in Schools and What to Do About It*. Markham, Ont.:
   Pembroke Publishers.

Chapter Five

Homophobia and
Diverse Sexual Orientation

Self-esteem is the comforting feeling that, for the moment at least, no
one is on to you.

—attributed to Oscar Wilde

Homophobia is generally defined as a fear and hatred of homosexuals.
However, as MacGillivray (2000) points out, this is a contradictory term
because a phobia is an irrational unreasoning fear, whereas homophobia is
learned behaviour. One cannot talk about homophobia without talking
about sexual orientation pertaining to homosexuality. Sexual orientation is
a deep personal truth. It is fundamental to one's being and, as such, is
fixed and immutable. Sexual orientation is part of a young person's identity whether that identity is heterosexual, bisexual, lesbian, gay, or transgendered. It is also an avenue through which a significant number of individuals are oppressed. Most people subscribe to multiple identities, and
teaching and learning about equity in schools can include issues surrounding sexual orientation. To omit this is to make unrecognized and
voiceless a significant portion of individual identity.

While sexual orientation appears to be an issue for teachers, it is as
much of an issue, or even more so, for students. Through teaching about
sexual orientation and its permutations, teachers may promote an understanding and acceptance of homosexuality and may assist students in their
classes to accept themselves and others who may have been born gay.

Gay students may not be willing to come out of the closet, even in a
safe and comfortable environment, simply because they cannot take
that safe and comfortable environment with them wherever they go. As

a result, issues surrounding homophobia are most often identified by teachers even though these issues may be of concern among their students. What follows is an attempt to come to terms with issues surrounding diverse sexual orientations and homophobia, to reflect critically about and to focus discussions about homosexuality in the classroom. Everywhere, however, it seems that teachers are constantly reminded of the darker suspicions with which their choice of topics is often viewed. Issues of personal agendas or malicious intent are often raised, and teachers are often thoroughly scrutinized as they proceed about the daily business of their chosen careers. It is because of this extraordinary scrutiny that the following questions have arisen:

- Should teachers hide their sexual orientation if it does not conform to mainstream views?
- Should homosexual teachers speak openly about homosexuality and their private life in the classroom?
- How can school boards pursue anti-homophobia education when the boards' views clearly run counter to the religious faith of some of the students?
- Should religious students be allowed to leave the class during discussions of homosexuality?

Many teachers grapple with these issues on a daily basis. As parents become more supportive of their lesbian, gay, bisexual, or transgendered children, they may become more vigilant, vigorous, and vociferous in the protection of their childrens' basic human rights. Even though prohibition of bias on the basis of sexual orientation is contained in the Charter of Rights and Freedoms in Canada, teachers are often still afraid to discuss homosexuality in the classroom because of a perceived backlash from parents, administrators, students, or other teachers.

Some gay teachers are justifiably nervous about garnering negative attention. In school districts across the country, gay teachers may fear losing promotions, being unsuccessful in acquiring employment in their chosen field, or even losing careers they are currently successful in due to the issue of sexual orientation. By outing themselves, gay teachers may also face the risk of being targeted for violence by nonaccepting students, parents, and the community at large.

Despite the enormous risks, some gay teachers have managed to broach the topic of homosexuality with their students and have succeeded in developing among their students a positive attitude of acceptance toward sexual orientation. The following article, one student's burning issue, reveals that although there have been some small successes in overcoming homophobia, there is still much more that can be done before teachers can rest assured that everyone is aware of the power differentials invoked by the exclusion of differently gendered and homosexual individuals. Here is Matthew's view of homophobia:

Homophobia in Our Schools: What's Being Done?

Gay and lesbian youth are three times more likely to commit suicide than their straight peers. Thirty percent of all completed youth suicides are committed by homosexual youth. Approximately 70 percent of gay young men and 85 percent of young lesbians have reported using alcohol and/or other drugs on a regular basis (Riddle 1996). These facts are shocking and disturbing to me, both as an educator and a gay man. I have chosen to examine homophobia in our schools as my burning issue. I chose this topic not only because of the facts above, which clearly demonstrate the low level of tolerance and support for gay youth, but also because of my personal experience of "coming out" as a young person. I came out when I was 18, after leaving high school. I did not feel comfortable with my gay identity, and I spent a lot of energy hiding my true feelings and pretending to be something I was not. I believe that it was the lack of visibility and support in our schools as well as a lack of positive gay role models and images that delayed my acceptance of my sexuality and caused me to feel alone and miserable for most of my teen years. The difficulties and issues facing gay youth will be discussed. I will also summarize some of the changes that have taken place regarding homophobia and heterosexism in schools and what still needs to be done to make schools safe for our lesbian, gay, bisexual, and transgendered youth.

Gay and lesbian youth often feel like they need to pretend to be someone they are not. I know that I felt that way when I was younger, and I always felt that I was "different," but without having a name to put to my difference I was confused and unhappy. In addition to the usual adjustments of growing up, starting or going through puberty, gaining more privileges and more responsibilities, and starting to develop strong emotional feelings for others, gay and lesbian youth must also incorporate their identity and difference into all of those growing experiences. They have to deal with their emotional and sexual feelings for members of the same sex while trying to develop their identity as future adults. Many homosexual adults recall having strong feelings for members of the same sex during elementary school (Anderson 1994). Often these youth must keep their feelings to themselves for fear of reprisals in the form of name-calling, teasing, and physical violence. A poll taken in 1992 said that 86 percent of high school students would be very upset if classmates called them lesbian or gay (Anderson 1997). The words "faggot" and "dyke" and "queer" ring out on playgrounds across the country, often with no consequence or discussion by teachers or administrators. More disturbing, 41 percent of lesbian and gay youth suffer violence from their families, peers, and strangers (Edwards 1997). Although this violence and harassment is going on, most school administrators believe that programs already in place are adequate to deal with the problem. In fact, many do not believe that programs targeted toward reducing homophobia are necessary, as they sing the popular refrain "there are no gays in our schools" (Anderson 1994). The very fact of the invisibility of this sexual minority should indicate how uncomfortable students are and how unsafe they feel coming out in school.

The issue of homophobia does not only affect gay and lesbian youth. Millions of children are raised by gay or lesbian parents. Even more have a family member or friend who identifies as lesbian or gay. The epithets and teasing hurt these children as well and keep them from sharing their lives and experiences honestly and completely. At such a young age, children are already learning that they must keep secrets and lie and hide things that are important to them. This is simply unacceptable. But what can be done? What will it take to make a positive change that will allow an acceptance and appreciation for diversity? The answer is, a lot.

Teachers, administrators, students, and parents must all be a part of the process of making our schools safe for gay and lesbian youth. Teachers need to be educated about the myths and realities of lesbians and gays. They also need to make a stand when they hear homophobic slurs and teasing. They need to include gay and lesbian issues in their curriculum. This should not be a time-consuming or expensive proposition. Doing something as simple as including a unit on the gay rights movement while studying civil rights in history or reading a story that involves two parents of the same sex in elementary school is a beginning. Inclusive language and a zero-tolerance approach to homophobic behaviour is vital, so that youth dealing with sexuality issues can feel comfortable being themselves in school. Teachers who are gay or lesbian should feel comfortable discussing their partners and home life in the context of discussions about family life. Administrators must support the teachers 100 percent, for there will certainly be questions raised by concerned parents. Administrators should be able to explain that the issue goes beyond accepting our gay and lesbian youth to acceptance of diversity in general. It would be a disservice to our youth as a general population not to educate them about homosexuality, as it is a guarantee that at some point in their lives they will come across a gay or lesbian person, and they need to know how to respond appropriately and deal with those people as just that, people. Parents need to be supportive and open-minded and deal with their own stereotypes and misconceptions around gay people. The most important thing for parents to understand is that equity policies and a gay and lesbian curriculum is not intended to convert or recruit their children to become gay or lesbian. The need for inclusion of gay and lesbian issues is to deal with the horrible abuse and self-abuse that goes on because of homophobia and heterosexism (heterosexism occurs when people assume that everyone is heterosexual and includes using exclusive language such as husband/wife, boyfriend/girlfriend). And students need to feel comfortable talking about their lives, their feelings, and their confusion. Students should feel comfortable asking questions and they should know that they will get an answer rather than having the issue ignored. Students also need to deal with their own stereotypes and ideas around homosexuality and they need to understand that homophobic behaviour is socially and legally unacceptable. Change is coming slowly, but it is coming.

As more and more people come to realize the detrimental effects of homophobia and heterosexism on our gay and lesbian youth, and on our society in general, changes are being made. School boards are including anti-homophobia policies in their equity policies and mission statements. Some teachers are including homosexual issues in their curriculum and pointing out the sexual orientation of certain famous figures in history and English. A few teachers have come out in their classroom, including elementary school, so that students can see positive gay role models. The benefits of this action include allowing the teachers to put all their energy into teaching rather than wasting energy hiding things or lying (Rensenbrink 1996). In June of 1999, the Toronto District School Board drafted a new equity policy that includes strong support for anti-homophobia work and inclusion and support for gay, lesbian, bisexual, and transgendered students. Even before this document was created, Toronto had a strong anti-homophobia policy. Services include individual counseling, support and advocacy, a facilitated discussion group for queer and questioning youth, classroom and schoolwide presentations on gay/lesbian/bisexual issues and anti-homophobia, support, counseling, and services for les/gay/bi parents and TDSB staff. These are definitely steps in the right direction, but more needs to be done. Other urban and rural schools and school boards also need sensitivity to this issue, for homosexual youth exist in these areas as well and often there is more of a stigma attached to being lesbian or gay in smaller communities. Furthermore, although the equity policy begins the process of establishing a firm anti-homophobia policy in this city, it will only go as far as educators and administrators are willing to take it. We need strong administrators and teachers to request services and workshops for their schools. We need teachers to feel more comfortable discussing homosexuality in their classes, and we need them to be firm and discuss the issue of homophobic slurs, teasing, and violence and let students know that behaviour of this sort will not be tolerated. We need parents to realize that anti-homophobia education and policy is important and necessary for young people and that no age is too young to begin teaching our youth about acceptance and respect for diversity. We need them to support the staff and to follow up our work at home and in their neighbourhoods. Finally, we need our students to be open minded, to realize that everyone is different, that being gay or lesbian is okay, that having gay or lesbian parents is good, and that using homophobic slurs and hate-related violence is absolutely not okay. And we need our gay and lesbian youth to be strong, to stand up in the face of ridicule and harassment and say that this is not okay. We need them to teach the teachers about their needs, about what they want and what they expect. This is not an easy request that we make of our youth or ourselves, but it is the only way that change is going to come about. The public education system must move on with the rest of the world and bring this issue out for discussion and education and teach tolerance, acceptance, and respect for diversity. I look forward to the challenge and the rewards of this journey that we, as a society, have begun.

References

Anderson, J. D. 1994. School climate for gay and lesbian students and staff members. *Phi Delta Kappan* 76, no. 2 (October): 151–154.

Anderson, J. D. 1997. Supporting the invisible minority. *Educational Leadership* 54, no. 7 (April): 65–68.

Edwards, Ann. 1997. Let's stop ignoring our gay and lesbian youth. *Educational Leadership* 54, no. 7 (April): 68–70.

Rensenbrink, C. W. 1996. What difference does it make? The story of a lesbian teacher. *Harvard Educational Review* 66, no. 2 (Summer): 257–270.

Riddle, Bob. 1996. Breaking the silence: Addressing gay and lesbian issues in independent schools. *Independent School* 55, no. 2: 38–47.

It has been said that homophobia is the last form of tolerated prejudice. Even for those who struggle with issues of tolerating a form of sexual expression that is totally foreign to one's own beliefs and practices, acceptance is not an endorsement of homosexuality. To understand, tolerate, and accept homosexuality as a difference in sexual orientation that is about as peculiar as eye colour or fashion sense does not mean that one embraces and practices homosexuality. It simply means that one has done the work of reflecting on whatever one's lived experiences may be concerning homosexuality and coming to terms with the fact that it is not contagious, it is not a choice, and that homosexuals are not necessarily pedophiles. It is this critical inquiry into the nature of sexual orientation issues that is necessary in order to develop an understanding of homosexuality. By inquiring into and understanding this issue, it becomes more possible to tolerate and to accept that homosexuality or diverse sexual orientations are not in and of themselves harmful, perverted, or degenerate. To accept this is to embrace the fear of what it may be and come to recognize homosexuality as it is.

EDUCATIONAL EQUITY FOR
QUESTIONING STUDENTS

The principles of democracy demand that gay, lesbian, bisexual, transgendered, and queer/questioning students, like all students, deserve social
justice, equal representation, and developmental support from educational
institutions. MacGillivray (2000) explains how differently sexually oriented students are currently denied the same educational opportunities accorded heterosexual students. Such denial is unjust and should be reme-
died.

Most societies are based on the a culture of heteronormativity, a culture
where heterosexuality is taken to be the norm. Because of this,
MacGillivray (2000) states that society's institutions are based on "het-
erologic," the idea that same-sex attraction is neither recognized nor acknowledged by the public or by social institutions. Resulting from this is
heterosexism and heterosexual privilege. Heterosexism refers to the belief
that everyone is or should be heterosexual, while heterosexual privilege
refers to privileges that heterosexuals take for granted and accept as normal without realizing that others are denied these privileges. Heterosexuals are privileged in that their relationships are accepted and affirmed by
every facet of the culture within which they live; for example, insurance
companies, property laws, tax returns, probate laws, and child custody issues, to name a few, resulting in a host of social, emotional, and economic
costs to differently sexually oriented individuals. The effect of this privileging serves to reinforce rigid gender stereotypes. However, by including
discussions of gender identity, sexual orientation, and discrimination
against those with diverse sexual orientations, schools may begin to de-
construct gender-role stereotypes that serve to limit all students. All youth
have the right to be provided with correct, accurate, and relevant information, no matter how controversial it may be considered to be.

IS HOMOPHOBIA AN ISSUE?

Few gay teachers risk being open about their sexual orientation for fear of
harassment, loss of job security, and a host of other threats to their health,
welfare, and safety. But the absence or misrepresentation of such models
impacts upon differently sexually oriented students who are attempting to

develop positive self-images and strong self-concepts, making it more difficult for these students to grow into healthy, mature adults.

But while schools have an obligation to treat all students in a socially just way, do schools have an obligation to explore the topic of homophobia and different sexual orientations with their students? If homophobia is not an issue in schools, is it fair to deal with it? Whatever the answer to this previous question may be, if it has become an issue, it must be dealt with. It is important to not politicize students regarding the issue of taking a stand regarding homophobia. To be "for it" or to be "against it" is to be politicized. To have a school policy that requires homophobia to be addressed is simply another example of policy driving the curriculum. In fact, the curriculum should be driven by students' needs or, at the very least, the perceptions of what students' needs are or represent. If issues surrounding homophobia are an issue, then teachers need to recognize the teachable moment.

Equally as important and delicate as broaching the topic of sexual orientation is the need to develop not only tolerance but acceptance of homosexuality. With all that we have learned about homophobia and homosexuality, if teachers merely attempt to teach tolerance, they are merely supporting or developing coping mechanisms within the students. In doing this, teachers are not teaching about differences, they are simply facilitating and reinforcing the existence of disabling stereotypes. To *accept* difference is to understand *why* the difference exists, and this involves research and study, which in turn, leads to a broader and more encompassing understanding—in short, a critical view.

How do you accept diversity in general instead of working through a personal agenda? Many of the issues surrounding homophobia are similar to those of bullying, including violence or symbolic violence toward homosexuals, exclusion, and the imposition of control. Consequently, many of the strategies presently in use for anti-bullying curricula are useful in developing a tolerance for sexual orientation that runs counter to the majority sexual orientation.

ADDRESSING HOMOPHOBIA IN
THE CLASSROOM AND AT SCHOOL

In order to move beyond homophobic reactions to a greater acceptance of different sexual orientations, numerous strategies can be developed. The following items are by no means exhaustive but represent a compilation of possibilities:

- Immediately addressing negative school-based incidents such as harassment, anti-gay insults, jokes, anti-gay graffiti, and labeling may help to prevent a tradition of homophobia from progressing.
- Adjusting language that implies or assumes that everyone is or should be heterosexual may be beneficial. For example, "partner" is more gender neutral than "boyfriend" or "girlfriend."
- Studies of histories of oppression may provide opportunities to discuss oppression related to sexual orientation.
- Including issues of sexual orientation and homophobic reactions in programs to prevent suicide, dropping out, pregnancy, drug abuse, and sexual abuse and harassment may also serve to raise the profile of sexual diversity.
- Improving library holdings that relate to sexual diversity, in both fiction and nonfiction genres, helps to raise the profile that diverse sexual orientation is not unusual, taboo, or something to be feared.
- Developing, providing, and advising about resources about sexual orientation may serve to reduce embarrassment and tension around such issues.
- Making materials and services visible and easily available can send out strong messages about inclusiveness and acceptance.

Most important, however, it is necessary to keep in mind that it is the teacher's values, beliefs, and perceptions toward these issues that will tend to determine students' reactions. Above all, the educators' attitudes and actions will determine how successfully students' attitudes toward diverse sexual orientations and homophobia can be challenged in order to develop a greater capacity for equity and social justice.

Programs that give all students an opportunity to develop an understanding in addressing issues of sexual orientation are often positive experiences for all interested youth as they provide social, emotional, and developmental support for questioning young people, be they gay, straight, or undecided. There are very few organizations for diversely oriented youth within society because most organizations are geared toward their adult counterparts. The school can serve an important function in asserting social and intellectual objectives pertaining to democratic and social justice issues. Just as racial and ethnic segregation prevents students from learning and growing from one another, so too do school practices that deny heterosexual and diversely sexually oriented people opportunities to learn more about themselves and to banish the stereotyping, prejudice, and discrimination that occurs as the result of the fear and hatred that is the fruit of ignorance.

The dilemma for educators is the problem of being caught between those who advocate and those who oppose the inclusion of issues and topics relating to diverse sexual orientations. The problem for educators continues to be how to be as inclusive as possible in creating a curriculum that values the voices of all members of the school community. While schools should not be allowed to advocate certain lifestyles, they should be allowed to provide information in a nonthreatening atmosphere, in a safe environment. According to MacGillivray (2000), information on sexual orientation and gender identities can be incorporated into the curriculum in a neutral manner without valorizing one lifestyle over another.

IMPLICATIONS FOR CLASSROOM PRACTICE

Discussions of diverse sexual orientation and homophobic reactions represent critical inquiry in action. Educators may choose to not only question their own assumptions, understanding, and preconceived notions of what it means to be gay or lesbian, bisexual, or transgendered, they also may wish to question the assumptions, understandings, and preconceptions of others. Such actions have implications for the classroom that may be profound and far-reaching.

Heterosexuality is strongly reinforced by the social practices and traditions of schools. While there are many opportunities to affirm heterosexual identities in school, there are few clubs or programs to support diversely sexually oriented youth, thus reinforcing the social isolation faced by these individuals. Positive role models, messages, and images about diverse sexually oriented individuals and groups of individuals are often absent or are deliberately silenced in school settings. This is not a matter of moral judgment but an issue of social justice. Rather than being systematically excluded, *systemic inclusion,* a process by which heterosexualism is reinforced, could also be extended to students of diverse sexual orientation. It is only in this way that any system can be truly termed inclusive.

School administrators and teachers often feel that sexuality, let alone homosexuality, is a topic they would sooner not have to deal with. Furthermore, it is often felt that teaching about homosexuality or diverse sexual orientations is advocating, or at least teaching values relating to, such topics. Also, educators may feel that discussing such topics in the classroom or at school may violate parents' and students' rights. While these are valid concerns, agreement on what they actually mean is difficult to achieve. Educators may wish to include or at least inform parents when information is being presented in the classroom and at school. Parental involvement, insofar as is possible, would be a positive way of keeping parents informed and aware of any potentially inflammatory emergent issues. Ideally, parents and teachers may find it beneficial to work together on in-class and at-home assignments. Unbiased and complete information and accurate statistics are essential so that instruction does not reinforce old stereotypes about sexual orientation. Accurate and timely information that will help break down myths and stereotypes can effectively be included in many sections of curricular offerings. Ample opportunities for students to ask questions are also important. To this end, it may be beneficial to have an anonymous question box that can be used for question periods on a regular basis.

CONCLUSION

Could the responsibility for the nonacceptance of homosexuality be an issue that is the responsibility of the entire society? After all, homophobia is socially constructed and therefore, while it is not strictly a problem in our schools, as a societal problem it can take a particularly ugly and destructive form in schools, where students may be victimized at some of the most insecure and vulnerable stages in their lives. Challenging forms of oppression and prejudice is the responsibility of everyone placed in positions of trust and caring for students, and indeed, for any member of society.

But whose problem is it anyway? Is it the problem of the gay student who fears disclosure? Is it a concern of the gay teacher who wishes respect and understanding? Or is it a social issue? An important reason for gay teachers to come out of the closet is that gay students may benefit from positive gay role models in their lives. In this way, issues raised by sexual orientation are no different than the issues raised by feminist liberation movements, which still actively search for appropriate role models for women in positions of power to emulate.

The reality is that many gay students feel alone and have no one to turn to. This fact alone helps to explain the alarming rate of suicide among gays. This is an equity issue, and bisexual, lesbian, gay, and transgendered youths are arguably the most vulnerable students in the school. They require protection. All students are entitled to a safe, caring environment in which to learn. Therefore, it is important in schools and in society to move beyond homophobia, even to move beyond tolerance of sexual orientation toward acceptance not only of homosexuality, bisexuality, and transgenderism, but of all points of difference between individuals and the society within which we live.

Debates about what we should or should not be teaching in schools continue to confound policymakers, educators, and politicians. However, in general, and as a general rule, this may be seen as an opportunity to consider that true liberal democracy is best served by a social justice perspective that will not allow opponents of inclusion, whether they be in the majority or minority, to dictate to schools what can or cannot be discussed. It continues to be a matter of the expression of voice, the exclusion of which cannot be viewed as a fair or natural stance.

IDEAS FOR STUDY

1. Using the homophobia and sexual orientation discussion template presented in the Supplementary Material, develop a forum for discussion around this topic. Students may find their own choice of articles for this purpose.
2. Based on the articles discussed in the question above, discuss in small groups how to deal with students who believe they may be homosexual.
3. What strategies can be used in order to address homophobia? Structure strategies around the school in general, the physical classroom, teacher

relationships with students, teaching and learning strategies, and class-room climate.
4. Does your institution or school board have policies relating to homo-phobia and diverse sexual orientation? Are such policies informative, and is it possible to implement them successfully?
5. What hidden messages relating to negative stereotyping of people of diverse sexual orientation occur in the media? Bring examples to class and be prepared to discuss the negative stereotyping and discuss ways in which this could be ameliorated.

SUPPLEMENTARY MATERIAL: DISCUSSION TEMPLATE

The following template may be used to discuss any topic in this volume. It may be adjusted as time and circumstances dictate. The objective of this format is to generate discussion and to promote deeper understanding of the topic being discussed. The articles for discussion may be drawn from the Recommended Reading section of this chapter.

1. Form students into groups of five.
2. Each group will decide on one presenter for each of the five articles.
3. Students will read one article to develop a summary and several thoughtful questions for discussion based on their article.
4. Appoint a timekeeper for the presentations.
5. Each person presents to the group for approximately five minutes.
6. The presenter then responds to questions or leads discussion on the article for another two or three minutes.
7. Conclude with a general discussion of the articles.

REFERENCE

MacGillivray, I. K. 2000. Educational equity for gay, lesbian, bisexual, transgen-dered, and queer/questioning students. *Education and Urban Society* 32, no. 3 (May): 303–323.

RECOMMENDED READING

Evans, K. 2002. *Negotiating the Self: Identity, Sexuality, and Emotion in Learning to Teach.* London/New York: RoutledgeFalmer.

Kozik-Rosabal, G. 2000 "Well, we haven't noticed anything bad going on," said the principal: Parents speak out about their families and schools. *Education and Urban Society* 32, no. 3 (May): 368–389.

Kumashiro. K. K., ed. 2001. *Troubling Intersections of Race and Sexuality: Queer Students of Color and Anti-Oppressive Education.* Lanham, Md.: Rowman & Littlefield Publishers.

McCaskell, T. 1999. Homophobic violence in schools. *Orbit: A Commentary on the World of Education* 29, no. 4.

Nahom, D., et al. 2001. Differences by gender and sexual experience in adolescent sexual behaviour: Implications for education and HIV prevention. *Journal of School Health* 71, no. 4 (April): 153–157.

Schneider, M. E., and R. E. Owens. 2000. Concern for lesbian, gay, and bisexual kids: The benefits for all children. *Education and Urban Society* 32, no. 3 (May): 349–367.

Chapter Six

Sexism and Feminist Issues in Teaching: Unpacking Inequity

Looking back at your life, you will see that moments which seemed to be great failures followed by wreckage were the incidents that shaped the life you have now.

—Campbell (1991, 38)

Addressing sexism and gender-equity issues will always meet with resistance, regardless of the setting, because people in general become uncomfortable when the status quo is questioned and perhaps reevaluated, resulting in the redistribution of power. However, such issues are important for teachers to address regardless of the opposition that may be faced. Feminist issues have been prominent among social justice issues during the past century. Anti-feminist activities have been acknowledged as a form of institutionalized oppression. Perhaps because they were among the first of a multitude of social justice issues to be highlighted in the public consciousness, feminist issues have been a source of constant tension between the sexes. Or perhaps they have received a rough ride because approximately half of any population is made up of women.

Because feminism was one of the first causes to be championed in the social changes of the 1970s, it may have suffered from a lack of previous role models. In fact, some changes desired by feminists may have been successfully engineered at the expense of issues near and dear to their male counterparts. This is not to say that feminist issues are not justified, but it is an attempt to recognize that while men and women are or should be equal, they are not necessarily the same in terms of their equality. This

91

is precisely what equity is about, the recognition of equal rights among diverse individuals.

This bid for parity has taken a long time, perhaps because those in power, the men, have relinquished their superior financial, educational, and dubious cultural capital only reluctantly. Unfortunately, many of the inequities of the past century remain with us today as women, and some men, continue the struggle to ensure that feminist issues are kept in the public eye. There are many fronts to this struggle, one of which is about equality, equity, and parity, but there is another struggle that has not received the attention that it should. That is the struggle to not valorize one prejudice above another. The feminist vision of equality, equity, and parity cannot be realized at the expense of masculine, or any other social justice, issues. Neither can men continue to dismiss serious feminist issues as insignificant, for that amounts to little more than burying their heads in the sand. Feminist issues are here to stay and will not dissolve into thin air any more than women will be content to resume their previous places as citizens second to men.

Conflict regarding this social justice issue continues to be waged in many arenas — on the home front, at work, in courts of law, and, unfortunately, in our classrooms. Anti-feminist practices are not necessarily overt or even conscious practices. Many of them occur as a result of acculturation and training. Such comments as "You run like a girl!' or "There, there. Big boys don't cry" serve to underline how systemic this issue is. The following journal entry, written by Hillary during the first practicum of her professional development year, reveals not only how difficult sexist tendencies are to eliminate, how pervasive they are in society, and how both genders indulge in sexist behaviour, but also how difficult it is to come to terms with adequate, appropriate, and equitable solutions. Here is one teacher candidate's reflection:

Something happened today that really made me think about how teachers may unconsciously encourage gender stereotypes. I was at my Student Teacher Education Program practicum and it was about lunch time. The teacher has a tradition of asking trivia questions for treats such as cookies in the spare moments of the day. (I think this is such a great idea.) He asks questions about history, current events, politics, popular culture and so on, which really gets the kids thinking and having fun at the same time. The teacher had just asked a question about football and a boy had answered.

The girls started chanting for him to ask a "girl question." He responded by asking, "Can you name a supermodel?"

My jaw just dropped that a teacher would automatically assume that a girl would *know* the answer. I again was shocked to think that he expected me, a female, to automatically care about the occupants of the fashion models' world. I pictured myself later, in that same situation, and what I would have done differently. I would have stopped the class and asked them, "What is a 'girl question' or a 'boy question,' for that matter?" Or I would have asked a question concerning great female accomplishments or about historical women (such as what famous women ruled the wealthy empire of Egypt). I am still not sure which approach would be better.

Feminist issues include a multitude of problems that are all equally important. These subthemes run the gamut from sexual orientation to race, colour, ethnic issues, and eating disorders to issues of religion, class, poverty, and social stratification (Beck 1989). It is essential to recognize that while these are all concerns of feminist theory and they all have their place among the myriad of feminist issues, what is an issue to one woman may not be an issue to another. A real and concrete issue such as poverty to a single female parent may be an abstraction to another. Consequently, none of these issues can be dismissed, not by men and not by women who do not suffer from the plight afflicting other women. At the same time, however, it can bring together people who differ in other respects but share the common experience of sexism.

EATING DISORDERS

Many issues regarding feminism have received attention in the past and continue to do so in the present. While these concerns continue to require attention, other important issues such as eating disorders, which affect women in far greater numbers than men, have received little attention except as distinct from feminist issues. Because of the "display ethic" that women need to appear as attractive as possible, eating disorders are a primarily feminine issue, perhaps resulting from the narrowing of one's access to power to the only thing that one really can control, food intake. Teachers are often unaware of students who are having difficulties with eating disorders and that they are a potentially lethal and desperate cry for assistance. A lack of sensitivity to such issues or a fear of not knowing how to approach them makes dealing with eating disorders a doubly difficult undertaking. Here is one student teacher's burning issue on the topic:

An Investigation of Eating Disorders

I would like to address eating disorders in my burning issue because I had an incident with one of my Grade 6 students last year which made me realize how unprepared and unknowledgeable in this area I was. Through the years I've known different people who have had or have eating disorders but I never really felt that it was my place to say anything. Quite frankly, I wouldn't have known what to do if someone had admitted to an eating disorder or known how to confront someone who I knew was taking laxatives, or purging. Not having an eating disorder background I didn't recognize or clue in when I saw a girl or girls getting sick in a restaurant bathroom. I would just simply think someone was sick. However, last year everything changed. I was teaching a class one afternoon when one of the vice principals called me out of my classroom. He had said that he needed my help getting one of the girls out of the bathroom because she was sick. Assuming she was just sick, I started talking to her, asking if she was okay, if she was dressed, or if she could open the door. The vice principal insisted that she needed to come out. I told the student that I was going to open the door (with "special" keys). The student then opened the door, coming out looking rather frazzled and dazed. The vice principal then confronted the student, asking her if she had heard about anorexia nervosa, and that maybe Miss O. would have to talk to her about it. The vice principal then told me that the student had been doing this for the past three days. I was flabbergasted. First of all, I had not clued in that this student was not just sick and that she may be well on her way to a flourishing eating disorder, let alone any idea of what I would or should say if I was to have a "talk" with her. Fortunately, when I came to school the next day, the office told me that someone else was looking after the student, spending time with her and eating with her. Now that I've done some research into this issue, I hope that this student has gotten professional help and won't slide back into some of her old routines.

As my area of specialization is physical and health education, I will probably need to teach units on body image and self-esteem, which are units in Grades 6 and 7. If these units are in the curriculum to help prevent eating disorders, then they seem to be coming too late. My student needed prevention strategies before the end of Grade 6, as did one of my associate teacher's Grade 4 students. Therefore, my focus is on eating disorders and how to prevent them in the elementary grades.

What Is an Eating Disorder?

An eating disorder is a psychiatric illness with specific criteria that are outlined in the *Diagnostic and Statistical Manual* (DSM-IV) published by the American Psychiatric Association.

Approximately 1 out of every 100 adolescent girls develops anorexia nervosa, a dangerous condition in which people can literally starve themselves to death. One in 10 cases leads to death from starvation, cardiac arrest, other medical complications, or suicide (Piran, Levine, and Steiner-Adair 1999, xviii).

Another 2 to 5 out of 100 young women develop bulimia nervosa, a pattern of eating followed by behaviours such as vomiting, taking laxatives or diuretics (water pills), or overexercising to rid the body of food or calories consumed.

Binge-eating disorder, characterized by frequent episodes of uncontrolled eating, is probably the most common eating disorder. It occurs in 10 to 15 percent of mildly obese people (U.S. Department of Health and Human Services Office on Women's Health 1999).

In contrast to eating disorders, disordered eating refers to troublesome eating behaviours, such as restrictive dieting, bingeing, or purging, which occur less frequently or are less severe than those required to meet the full criteria for the diagnosis of an eating disorder. Many studies show that disordered eating behaviours begin as early as 8 years of age with complaints about body size or shape.

Most people diet at least some time in their lives, but when the dieting becomes obsessive it could be an eating disorder.

Implications/Effects

A review by the Tufts University School of Nutrition Science and Policy concludes that undernutrition—even in its "milder" forms—during any period of childhood can have detrimental effects on the cognitive development of children (Tufts University School of Nutrition Science and Policy 1998). Undernutrition has an impact on students' behaviour, school performance, and overall cognitive development. Hunger causes irritability, a decreased ability to concentrate, nausea, headaches, and lack of energy. These symptoms imply shorter attention spans and less ability to perform tasks. When students are not eating well, they become less active, more apathetic, and interact less with their surrounding environment, which affects their social interactions, inquisitiveness, and overall cognitive functioning. Being tired and more vulnerable to illnesses, these students are more likely to be absent from school. Additionally, studies have shown that people with anorexia nervosa report that 90 to 100 percent of their waking time is spent thinking about food, weight, and hunger; an additional amount of time is spent dreaming about food or having sleep disturbed by hunger (U.S. Department of Health and Human Services Office on Women's Health 1999). People with bulimia nervosa report spending about 70–90 percent of their total conscious time thinking about food and weight-related issues. People with disordered eating may spend about 20–65 percent of their waking hours thinking about food. By comparison, women with normal eating habits will probably spend about 10–15 percent of waking time thinking about food, weight, and hunger.

Physiologically and psychologically, students with disordered eating or eating disorders are severely limited in their ability to learn or interact with classmates and teachers. Hindered in interacting with peers and teachers, people with eating disorders become isolated in dealing with problems and can become difficult to be around. Despite these problems, many people with disordered eating or eating disorders go untreated and eventually become functioning members of society, although never *healthy* or fully *functioning* members of society, and they may never meet their full potential because their preoccupation takes up much of their energy. A significant number never reach adulthood because they die of starvation or other medical complications.

Application for the Classroom

The prevalence and seriousness of disordered eating make it an important issue to address in the classroom. Although there have been a number of different strategies used to prevent eating disorders and disordered eating, some of the educational approaches have been shown to do more harm than good (O'Dea and Maloney 2000). Some of these approaches are programs that provide information about eating disorders, particularly programs led by recovered eating disorder patients, or programs that glamorize, normalize, or treat food and nutrition issues negatively by referring to "good," "bad," and "junk" foods.

The most successful approach is the Health Promoting Schools Framework. The framework outlines requirements for a planned and sequential health education curriculum across all age groups and the need for intersectoral and cross-curricula. An example of this concept includes focusing on dieting prevention in health education classes (skill development to reduce the influence of peer-group pressure), English classes (the impact of persuasive advertising), and science (normal composition of fat in the human body). Some Canadian schools have adapted the Health Promoting Framework. However, cross-curricular activities become more difficult when students are on a rotary system. Addressing disordered eating and eating disorders becomes more practical to address in the junior band when the homeroom teacher can ensure that cross-curricular activities will be carried out. It is also an important age to start to recognize and discourage disordered eating as children as young as 8 are starting to show signs of disordered eating. The Harvard Eating Disorders Center reports that in a study of children 8 to 10, approximately half of the girls and one-third of the boys were dissatisfied with their size (Harvard Eating Disorders Center 1999; Collins 1991).

Although units on self-esteem and body image are not generally taught until Grades 6 and 7, the Ontario Health Curriculum includes expectations of healthy eating practices and heredity as they relate to body size and shape in Grade 4. An excellent resource for teaching this part of the curriculum is

Kathy Kater's *Healthy Body Image: Teaching Kids to Eat and Love Their Bodies Too!* The resource uses a cross-curricular approach, integrating health, science, media studies, art, and social studies. The guide is intended for Grades 4 to 6 and is age appropriate for these grades. Some of the lessons could be done in the intermediate division.

Another excellent resource is *Every BODY Is a Somebody* by the Body Image Coalition of Peel. The guide includes lessons and activities on the media and critical thinking, self-esteem and body image, the body's resistance to dieting, healthy eating and an active lifestyle, stress management, and relationships. I have found this resource to be very useful in teaching assertiveness and resisting peer pressure. Other teachers have found the body-image lessons to be very constructive for Grade 6 to 8 students. However, this resource would be more effective if it is augmented with science lessons on how heredity effects body size and shape along with activities that would help students accept their hereditarily determined size and shape. This resource links the activities to the Ontario Health Curriculum expectations for Grades 6 to 10, although some of the activities could be done in Grades 4 and 5. Supplementing would be required for a unit on body image in Grades 4 and 5.

Strategies that all teachers can adapt using the Health Promoting Framework include:

- Reducing ideals about slender bodies, prejudices against fat and over-weight people, the centrality of body weight/shape, talk of good versus bad foods, negative body image, low self-esteem, teasing about weight and shape, gender stereotyping.
- Increasing healthy eating, healthy exercise, critical thinking, skepticism about dieting, multifaceted identity, problem-oriented coping skills, assertive communication skills, listening skills.

If a teacher suspects a child has an eating disorder or disordered eating she or he should consult with other staff members. Ask colleagues if they have noticed any of the same behaviours and if they know anything about the situation. If, for example, you notice a student is habitually staying in the washroom for long periods of time after lunch, ask the office if they are aware of any medical problem this student may have. If there is not a medical problem and your colleagues have been noticing similar behaviours, then confront the student and notify the student's parents. The office and school counselor should be told about the situation. When you or another staff member are confronting the student, focus on your concerns about her or his health and functioning, don't focus on weight loss or body size. The student and the parents should be referred to a professional who has experience working with patients who have eating disorders. The National Eating Disorder Information Centre (NEDIC) can refer people to such professionals. NEDIC recommends that schools have policies on eating disorders. Unfortunately, not all schools have such policies. NEDIC can be reached by telephone at (416) 340-4156, by fax at (416) 340-4736, or by e-mail via their website (www.nedic.on.ca).

Eating disorders are clearly not an issue of noncompliance but are psychiatric illnesses that include anorexia nervosa, bulimia, and binge-eating disorder. Students suffering from one or more of these disorders are seriously limited in their ability to interact and learn. One preventative measure that has been successfully employed is the Health Promoting Schools Framework, which outlines a planned and sequenced health education curriculum across all grades. Any teacher who is concerned that a student is suffering from an eating disorder is advised to consult with colleagues, administrators, and counselors. The National Eating Disorder Information Centre acts as a referral service for students, parents, and teachers.

ADDRESSING SEXISM IN THE
CLASSROOM AND AT SCHOOL

The term "sexism" is usually used to cover both inappropriate beliefs and attitudes in relation to the sexes and discrimination against people on the basis of sex (Beck 1989). In his chapter entitled "Sexism" in his book *Better Schools*, Beck (1989) notes that schools promote sexism both informally — through organization, atmosphere, comments, and gestures — as well as formally—through curricular and instructional activities. Sexism is harmful in at least three ways:

- Through promoting inaccurate stereotypes of males and females that result in inappropriate expectations and behaviours
- Through promoting the view that females are usually inferior to males, leading to inappropriate attitudes and actions
- Though promoting discrimination against females, usually in favour of males

Such practices are harmful to both sexes because the exploiter is negatively affected by her or his own oppressive practices. Beliefs that differentiated treatment is justified because women constitute the "fairer" or "weaker" sex are also inappropriate. Such genetic explanations, as with race and ethnicity, should be a matter of last, rather than first, resort, since most differences between male and female are culturally and psychologically determined. Many of the differences between females and males can also be explained in terms of differentiated access to power. This does not mean to imply that if women had equal access to power that they would begin to behave like males. In fact, there is growing evidence that a more "feminine" approach is required, at least to a degree, in those larger societal and global settings where males dominate (Beck 1989). Girls are often subjected to sexual bias while at school. There may be a parallel here with social class and schooling even though girls, unlike students of lower socioeconomic status, do relatively well at school.

Teachers play many roles and hold positions of privilege and power through the transmission of knowledge, skills, and attitudes to their students, who are often at their most impressionable. Teachers must be vigilant about what it is that they are teaching and modeling because of the cumulative effect of gender inequity. Sexism can seriously affect the development of young people emotionally, socially, and professionally.

IMPLICATIONS FOR CLASSROOM PRACTICE

An inclusive classroom environment is essential in order for students to feel safe in asking questions and offering information about gender, equity, sexism, and feminist issues. Classroom learning environments can be structured to allow choice, student involvement, sharing, freedom to explore, and flexibility. Teachers may effect these changes by connecting contributions, respecting opinions, and allowing students a voice. Within the classroom, the Toronto District School Board, for example, suggests the following:

- Set limits that state that no aspect of a student's identity is ever an acceptable reason for privilege, exclusion, or violence, symbolic or otherwise.
- Intervene immediately and determine reasons for conflict. The three-step rule of "Stop!," "I (*message*)," and "How would you feel if . . ." help to encourage critical thought and discussion.
- Support the target of non-discrimination. Discuss with the class how it feels to be included or excluded.
- Assist students to develop an ease with and respect for issues of gender equity.
- Model inclusive, nondiscriminatory language for your students.
- Include both boys and girls in discussions, activities, and decision-making.
- Allow equal time for both boys and girls to express their opinions, attitudes, and feelings.
- Encourage all students to speak up in a voice suitable to the occasion.
- Develop independence by allowing students to work through things themselves. Assist only after they have given it a fair try.
- Provide students with opportunities to be both leaders and followers.

Beck (1989) notes that in response to the challenge of continuing sexism in schools and in the job market, teachers may be seen as both a major obstacle to change and as a means by which change may be achieved. In counseling female students regarding career paths, teachers may take care to employ a dialogic approach that allows the student to determine the most satisfactory study and career path for the individual. The current emphasis on math, science, and technology as entry qualifications for occupations such as medicine, engineering, and business, for example, are not in keeping with the broad range of skills and abilities actually required in those occupations. Consequently, such admission requirements tend to steer high school students, particularly girls, toward specialization in subjects that are often against their inclinations. In order to gain acceptance to higher education, access to occupations with a humanities background are considered more suitable feminine pursuits, as opposed to more scientific orientations. Therefore, in addition to attempting to improve the career expectations of females, schools can teach against sexual prejudice and discrimination rather than emphasizing the differences between boys and girls. Attention can be paid to sexist messages in textbooks that use stereotypes and ignore the contributions that women have made to society. Beck comments that helping people to see that sexual bias is inappropriate is a task to which the school should devote considerable time, attention, and resources.

In order to accomplish such tasks in coeducational classrooms or same-sex classrooms, a major issue to contend with is the external issue of culturally approved models of masculine and feminine behaviour. A second major theme is the notion of credit and blame. For example, boys tend to credit themselves when they succeed and blame external influences when they fail. For girls, it is often the opposite; they tend to blame their own inability when they do poorly and credit luck or circumstance when they do well.

Dealing with feminist issues in schools is often an exercise in exclusion as one form of sexism often becomes valorized over another. For example, in her article, "Must Girl-Friendly Schools Be Girls-Only Schools?," Robertson (1997) suggests that the argument for "girls-only" schools is in conflict with principles of equity and that while it may be widely believed that low self-esteem is a chronic problem among adolescent girls, attempts to improve self-esteem may merely teach girls to value themselves despite the fact that they are female. Furthermore, the belief that conventional classrooms "silence" girls' voices is deemed a matter of reception rather than a problem of expression. Just as teachers have an obligation to ensure that girls' voices are expressed and heard, it is equally important for boys to learn to listen. Robertson also notes that while conventional wisdom indicates that girls receive an inferior science and math education, social class is actually a more significant predictor of school success than gender. Also, Robertson believes that charter schools invite elitism and tribalism and that while efforts to improve girls' education have made a difference, educators have been less successful in altering the beliefs and behaviours of boys and men.

Students may benefit from illustrating their understandings of sexism, in a variety of ways. "Educational play" can be facilitated through incorporating the performing arts, music, drama, and intellectual games and exercises. For example, students may use the Quotations about Women activity in the Ideas for Study section of this chapter to explore how other groups of women have been oppressed in both past and present times. While this activity may help in developing a growing awareness of feminist issues, many of the quotations are not simply anti-feminist, they are anti-male as well.

It may also benefit the entire class to acknowledge common needs of the class as a group. This may be accomplished in an atmosphere of respect for individual differences within a safe environment. Also, students may require additional time to produce results that they are satisfied with.

CONCLUSION

Gender inequity, sexism, and anti-female behaviour is a reality in schools and classrooms. This does not mean that teachers are guilty of perpetuating such inequity. These issues are complex and are layered by a multitude of other social justice issues. Effecting gender equity, anti-sexism, and inclusiveness in our schools is a necessary and worthy course of action in order to prevent such inequities from being internalized by students who, as adults, become victims or perpetuators of such behaviours, It is important that teachers challenge themselves to construct or review their equity practices and strategies to empower students to challenge and confront gender bias as they encounter it.

Such strategies can include attempts to balance power relations between the sexes, to treat each gender equitably and equally, and to acknowledge the power structures that give boys advantageous greater stimulus, support, and resources than girls. It is important to bear in mind that there is no one best strategy to use because all strategies depend on time, tone, and intent.

The school environment must also be assessed for inequitable practices. This may be accomplished, in part, by integrating women's experiences into the fabric of the curriculum. Sexual harassment policies may be enforced more diligently or developed where they are absent. As

Coulter (1996) suggests, it is not enough to teach students to overcome systemic barriers to equity; the very barriers themselves need to be challenged.

IDEAS FOR STUDY

1. Do the Quotations Activity with the entire class. A template is provided in the Supplementary Material section of this chapter.
2. See Beck (1989) and discuss how women and men are disadvantaged or negatively affected by sexism.
3. Role-play the following scenarios:

   • You suspect one of your students has an eating disorder. How will you approach the situation?
   • You overhear two of your Grade 4 students complaining about being overweight. They have decided to go on a diet. How will you handle this situation?

4. How can we, as teachers, educate our students about eating disorders in a way that would be both preventative and constructive?
5. Discuss the following in small groups and report back to the large group to further the discussion:

   • Do coeducational schools provide an inferior education for girls?
   • Are girls silenced intentionally or unintentionally in conventional classrooms?
   • Do single-sex schools encourage or discourage equity? How?

6. Do you believe that math and science classes can or should be gender segregated in regular intermediate schools similar to physical education?
7. How are women's issues currently dealt with in schools and how could such issues be dealt with more effectively? What strategies can be used to narrow the gender gap?
8. Thinking back on your own educational experience, can you recall having to study something that seemed totally irrelevant and meaning-

less? Was it the content, the method of teaching, or both content and method that was problematic? Discuss why this was an issue.

9. What strategies can teachers use to create as close to a bias-free class-room as possible?

SUPPLEMENTARY MATERIAL

Quotations Activity

The author acknowledge and thank students and faculty at OISE/UT for this activity. The objectives are as follows:

- To encourage students to question messages or comments regarding feminism.
- To demonstrate that sexism has a long and universal history.
- To understand that sexism has been condemned by many people, past and present.

The preparation is to create index cards containing quotes about women. Quotations can be found below. The procedure is as follows:

1. Divide students into groups of four.
2. Each group receives a different set of cards containing quotations about women.
3. The instructor places a chart on the wall showing a continuum of opinion (very positive to positive to neutral to negative to very negative).
4. Each group discusses their set of quotations and ranks them from very positive to very negative.
5. One group member reads at least one quotation aloud and places the quotation in the appropriate column on the chart, corresponding to the group's evaluation of the quotations.
6. After all the groups have completed this part of the exercise, the instructor asks if any of the quotations should be moved from one category to another.
7. When consensus is achieved, the instructor asks for observations and conclusions about how women have been perceived, past and present.

8. Students may write about one of the quotations to which they have had a strong positive or negative reaction and/or about how other messages they have received about feminism have had an influence on how they feel about gender and gender bias.

Quotations about Women

James Stephens, 1930: "Women are wiser than men because they know less and understand more."

Charlotte Whitton, mayor of Ottawa, 1962: "She must do twice as well as a man to be thought half as good. But it's not too hard for a woman to be twice as good as a man."

Sojourner Truth, 1851: "That man . . . says that women need to be helped into carriages, and lifted over ditches, and to have the best places everywhere. . . . Nobody ever helps me into carriages, or over mud puddles, or give me any best places, and aren't I a woman? I have plowed, and planted, and gathered into barns, and no man could head me—and aren't I a woman?"

Agnes MacPhail, 1925: "When I hear men talk about women being the angel of the home, I always, mentally at least, shrug my shoulders in doubt. I do not want to be the angel of any home; I want for myself what I want for other women, absolute equality. After that is secured, then men and women can take turns at being angels."

Election Act of the Dominion of Canada, 1867: "No woman, idiot, lunatic or criminal shall vote."

Lord Chesterfield, 1748: "Women are only children of a larger growth."

Oscar Wilde: "Wicked women bother one. Good women bore one."

Thomas Fuller, 1732: "A woman, a spaniel, a walnut tree. The more they're beaten the better they be."

Cheyenne proverb: " A nation is not conquered until the hearts of its women are on the ground."

Nellie McClung: "Never apologize, never explain. Just get the job done and let them howl."

John Wayne: "They have a right to work wherever they want to—as long as they have dinner ready when you get home."

St. Thomas Aquinas: "In her particular nature, woman is defective and misbegotten, for the active force in the male seed tends to the production of a perfect likeness in the masculine sex; while the production of woman is due to a weakness in the generative force or imperfection in the pre-existing matter or even from some external influences, for example, the humid winds from the South."

Aristotle: "We should look upon the female state as it were a deformity, although one that occurs in the ordinary course of nature."

Rebecca West: "People call me a feminist whenever I express sentiments that differentiate me from a doormat."

Trieu Thi Trinh: "My dream is to ride the tempest, tame the waves, kill the sharks. I want to drive the enemy away to save our people. I will not accept the fate of women who bow their heads and become concubines."

Zulu women warrior song: "Now you have offended women; now you have touched rock; now you will be crushed."

Chinese proverb: "Ugly wives and stupid maids are priceless treasures."

Chippewa chief, 1930: "Women are created for work. One of them can draw or carry as much as two men. They also pitch our tents, make our clothes, mend them, and keep us warm at night. . . . We absolutely cannot get along without them on a journey. They do everything and cost only a little; for since they must be forever cooking, they can be satisfied in lean times by licking their fingers."

Mohammed, Koran: "Your women are a field for you to cultivate, so go to your field as you will."

Orthodox Jewish daily morning prayer: "I thank thee, O Lord, that thou hast not created me a heathen . . . a slave . . . or a woman."

Denys Dionne, Quebec judge, 1990: "Rules are like women. They are meant to be violated."

Pope John Paul II: "I want to remind young women that motherhood is the vocation of women. . . . It is women's eternal vocation."

Hindu proverb: "Educating a woman is like handing a knife to a monkey."

English proverb: "A man is as old as he feels, and a woman as old as she looks."

Confucius: "Such is the stupidity of woman's character that it is incumbent upon her, in every particular, to distrust herself and to obey her husband."

Japanese proverb: "Beat your wife on the wedding day, and your married life will be happy."

Mencius, Chinese philosopher: "It does not belong to a woman to determine anything of herself, but she is subject to the Rule of the Three Obediences. When she is young, she has to obey her parents; when married, she has to obey her husband; when a widow, she has to obey her son."

Chinese proverb: "The glory of a man is knowledge, but the glory of the woman is to renounce knowledge."

REFERENCES

Beck, C. 1989. *Better Schools: A Values Perspective*. New York: Falmer Press.

Body Image Coalition of Peel. n.d. *Every BODY Is a Somebody*. Peel, Ont.: Body Image Coalition of Peel. Order online at http://www.bodyimagecoalition.org.

Campbell, J. 1991. Living in the world. In *A Joseph Campbell Companion*, ed. D. Osborn. New York: HarperCollins.

Collins, M. E. 1991. Body figure perceptions and preferences among preadolescent children. *International Journal of Eating Disorders* 10, no. 2: 199–208.

Coulter, R. P. 1996. Gender equity and schooling: Linking research and policy. *Canadian Journal of Education* 21, no. 4: 433–452.

Harvard Eating Disorders Center. 1999. Facts and findings. Harvard Eating Disorders Center website, www.hedc.org.

Kater, Kathy. n.d. *Healthy Body Image: Teaching Kids to Eat and Love Their Bodies Too!* Pleasantville, N.Y.: Sunburst Communications.

O'Dea, J., and D. Maloney. 2000. Preventing eating and body image problems in children and adolescents using the health promoting schools framework. *Journal of School Health* 70, no. 1: 18–21.

Piran, N., M. P. Levine, and C. Steiner-Adair, eds. 1999. *Preventing Eating Disorders: A Handbook of Interventions and Special Challenges*. Philadelphia: Brunner/Mazel.

Robertson, H.-J. 1997. Must girl-friendly schools be girls-only schools? Arguments against segregation based on sex. *Orbit: A Commentary on the World of Education* 28, no. 1: 2–7.

Tufts University School of Nutrition Science and Policy. 1998. Statement on the link between nutrition science and cognitive development in children. Boston: Center on Hunger, Poverty and Nutrition Policy.

U.S. Department of Health and Human Services Office on Women's Health. 1999. *The BodyWise Eating Disorders Information Packet for Middle School Personnel*. Washington, D.C.: U.S. Department of Health and Human Services.

RECOMMENDED READING

Beck, C. 1989. *Better Schools: A Values Perspective*. New York: Falmer Press.

Robertson, H.-J. 1997. Must girl-friendly schools be girls-only schools? Arguments against segregation based on sex. *Orbit: A Commentary on the World of Education* 28, no. 1: 2–7.

Chapter Seven

Diversity and Social Stratification

A critical curriculum does not supply answers. It supplies questions.

—Edelsky (1999, 31)

Issues of diversity and social stratification are complex and interrelated constructs. Classroom discussion on these topics may be challenging and warranted, but they are often confusing. Diversity and social stratification are not just about ethnicity but include issues of nationality, culture, wealth, education, physical ability, and others too numerous to mention here, including birthright, as important issues of social justice. While it may appear on the surface that such issues have long been dealt with and put aside, that is assuredly not the case. After some reflection, it may become clear that issues of diversity with regard to any society may have become institutionalized and may have often been accepted unquestioningly by members of the society. This can also be said of social stratification. Social stratification, or classism, is related to issues that limit certain individuals from full participation in the larger society through elitist practices. These practices may be manifested through inequalities in access to various forms of capital, such as cultural, financial, social, and educational capital, which result in disadvantaged or minority students becoming marginalized or viewed as at risk for failure within the school and the larger society and being consciously or unconsciously victimized by those in power over them.

These issues have never been resolved in the society at large, and for this reason it is incumbent upon the educator to not only be aware of these inequities but to employ policies, practices, and procedures that promote the acceptance of diversity while at the same time minimizing the effects of social stratification. Unfortunately, these issues, like many others, may suffer from having their profiles raised in the sense that once issues of inclusion and exclusion are recognized to be problematic, it becomes unpopular in the larger society to voice unsympathetic comments. Such issues then assume a deeper, more sinister aspect. Active discrimination can be dealt with through legal and social channels, but prejudice may remain deep seated and be virtually impossible to change. Over time, such issues may become institutionalized and become almost invisible as they assume the perspective of systemic, cultural, and social norms.

It is unusual to have a person from the uppermost ranks of the social elite talk about social stratification in the vein of critical inquiry. To do so would be to admit that the individual speaks from a position of power and privilege. It is also unusual for individuals and groups of individuals who command such power to want to share that power with those less fortunate than themselves. In fact, the opposite is true. Due to the capitalist nature of society, we have built a society based on a hierarchy of wealth (Hale 1994). As a result, privileged individuals no longer see that they are privileged but often regard others who do not have the same or adequate (to their minds) cultural, financial, educational, physical, or social capital as those they regard as base, poor, stupid, unfit, or uncouth. The privileged among us, as the dominant culture, set the standard for others to (unsuccessfully, for the most part) achieve.

Issues of social stratification are compounded by issues of diversity, simply because diverse populations imply differences in cultural, financial, educational, physical, or social capitals, not to mention differences in work ethic, values, beliefs, creeds, and religions. It is for these reasons that diversity and social stratification are important topics for all educators. Only by addressing these topics can people begin to see the limitations that they and their society place on others who are less fortunate, both within the mainstream culture of that society and beyond it. In an article in the *Globe and Mail* (2000), Will Kymlicka commented on legislative frameworks designed to recognize minorities within the Canadian society:

> The 20th century will be remembered as a century of wars, hot and cold, between states. The 21st century is likely to be a century of wars—within states, as ethnic minorities take up arms against the state. The portents are

already with us: Chechnya, East Timor, Kosovo, Sudan, Kashmir, Rwanda. The trend is so widespread, some observers call it the Third World War.

Canada has avoided the violence that has plagued other multi-ethnic countries. However, we've had to continually adapt and innovate to meet the challenge of accommodating diversity while respecting individual rights and maintaining stable political institutions.

Consider immigration. Prior to the 1960s, we expected immigrants to assimilate; indeed, we tried to keep out any groups seen as incapable of assimilation. Now that means learning one or both official languages and adopting liberal democratic values; once it also meant becoming indistinguishable from native-born citizens in their style of speech, clothes, diet, political views, work habits, family size and leisure activities. Not so long ago, it was un-Canadian if immigrants were too visibly "ethnic."

We repudiated this approach in 1971, when Canada became the first country to adopt a federal multiculturalism policy. We now view it as natural for immigrants to cherish and express their ethnic heritage and identity, and we expect public institutions, such as schools, hospitals, police and the media institutions designed to accommodate the beliefs and practices of British and French settlers—to accommodate the beliefs and practices of immigrant groups.

We were the first to constitutionally entrench multiculturalism, but others followed, including Australia, New Zealand, Sweden, and the Netherlands. A government-sponsored commission in Britain has just recommended the adoption of a Multiculturalism Act there. The United States has no official multiculturalism policy at the federal level, but policies exist at the state and local levels. Many observers believe that a multiculturalism policy would help solve the problem of violence against "foreigners" in countries such as Germany (against the Turks), or the Czech Republic (against the Roma).

In negotiating issues of heritage and rights, Canada has also been innovative concerning the Quebecois. After the Plains of Abraham, the British perceived danger in a minority group that thinks of itself as a separate "nation," and they made concerted efforts to deprive the French of this sense of minority nationhood. Things changed with the Confederation agreement of 1867, which recognized that the Quebecois would continue to exist as a separate society, with their own language and institutions, into the indefinite future. The most important way the Confederation manifested this acceptance of minority nationhood involved the decision to create a sub-unit—the province of Quebec—in which the French would be a local majority, thereby exercising significant self-government.

This was arguably the first time in any Western democracy when a territorial sub-unit was deliberately created to enable minority self-government. The idea of accommodating national minorities through territorial autonomy is now widespread: Witness Scotland and Wales in the U.K., Puerto Rico in the United States, Catalonia and the Basque Country in Spain, Flanders and Wallonia in Belgium, South Tyrol in Italy, the Aland Islands in Finland.

Indeed, it may be the only feasible approach for those countries in Eastern Europe, the Middle East or the Third World that contain powerful, sometimes violent minority nationalisms, such as Georgia (for the Abkhaz and Ossetians), Turkey (for the Kurds), Nigeria (for the Ogoni), and China (for Tibet).

A third innovation concerns the treatment of Aboriginal peoples. Again, the original goal of the British colonial governors and then the Canadian state was assimilation: They sought to strip Aboriginal peoples of their lands, and to "civilize" them—by eliminating the legal, political and educational institutions by which they had governed themselves, and replacing them with paternalistic rule.

But since the early 1970s, there has been a commitment, mandated by the Supreme Court and entrenched in the Constitution, to uphold treaties with Aboriginals, to recognize customary law and property rights, to negotiate new treaties and land claims, and to restore self-"government, including control over areas such as education, health care, resource development," and policing.

Canada was the first Western country to create a legislative framework for negotiating new treaties and land claims, and to constitutionally recognize indigenous rights—ahead of similar developments for the Aborigines in Australia, the Maori in New Zealand, the Sami in Scandinavia, and indigenous peoples throughout Latin America. The UN has suggested this approach would help resolve violent uprisings of indigenous peoples in Bangladesh, the Philippines and Mexico.

Canadians are surprised to hear that our policies have been so influential; we don't regard them as successes. The condition of Aboriginals is deplorable, Quebec almost seceded in 1995, multiculturalism remains controversial—and Canadian minorities sometimes doubt whether the larger society has really changed its attitudes. The majority, by contrast, feels that they have gone above and beyond the call of duty in accommodating minorities, and is hurt that minorities are not more grateful. To paraphrase P. G. Wodehouse, if Canadians are not actually disgruntled about these policies, they are far from gruntled.

Why, then, are our innovations adopted elsewhere? Whenever I travel abroad to discuss "the Canadian model," there are two aspects of our experience that other countries admire. The first concerns process. Canada has a legal framework for discussing issues of diversity. Policies of multiculturalism, federalism, arid Aboriginal rights give the relevant groups a seat at the table, and constitutional legitimacy to their identities and interests. Many countries have no framework for the majority and minorities to sit down and discuss how to live together. Our deliberations are often strained, but we do develop policies consensually.

The second concerns values. Canada has developed a political and legal culture that combines a commitment to universal values with recognition of diversity. In countries like the United States or France, people have a stark choice: Citizenship must either be based on universalistic values of freedom, equality, democracy and human rights that apply uniformly to all citizens, or it must be based on respect for particularistic identities—but not both.

The Canadian experience suggests this is a false choice. Canadian citizenship is, indeed, grounded in universalistic values of freedom, equality, democracy and human rights. Our consensus on these values cuts across ethnic, linguistic and religious lines. Polls show that we are just as committed to these values as citizens in the United States and France; we promote them in our schools, ask immigrants to accept them as a condition of citizenship, and expect the Supreme Court to uphold them.

In the past, our implementation of these values was stained by illiberal assumptions about the inferiority of other groups and cultures. As we head into the 21st century, we are building new models of citizenship that uphold universal values of democracy and human rights, while simultaneously respecting the various languages, cultures and identities that exist in Canada. The approach is by no means uniquely Canadian. But we have played a significant role in developing and diffusing it.

While not all minorities feel they have been fairly treated, the mainstream dominant culture believes that this framework is based on values of freedom, justice, and human rights. Presented below is one preservice student's view of how preservice education programs could be improved to be more inclusive of other cultures and those who may feel excluded by society.

Jeewan Chanicka, a preservice student who graduated in the spring of 2003, has agreed to allow us to use his burning issue essay, entitled to illustrate some of the issues present in the current system of schooling. He offers suggestions for improving matters:

Anti-Discrimination Pedagogy

Semester 1, 2002

Today was my preservice music class and I was extremely excited about going. After all I love to sing and I plan to learn to play a new musical instrument this year too! The class started out great as we eased into different activities. However, as I looked at the various strands of music that the students were expected to know about, I realized that the majority (5 out of 7) of the types of music was all Western-based.

I have no issue with Western music but I looked at the list and I was forced to ask myself what am I indirectly saying to my students when I teach primarily Western music and ignore other types of music that reflect their cultures as well. I further thought about my Grade 8 class, many of whom came from quite diverse backgrounds, and how they would feel. Would I be legitimizing their social location or would I be marginalizing these students even more?

I tried to put myself in their position . . . there were only two places that called for diverse music. One of the strands would examine music from indigenous cultures and the last one, music of the world.

Being in a research group on anti-racism encouraged me to think about a book, *Removing the Margins* (Dei 2000), which focused on the need for curriculum to be inclusive. The book suggested that individuals should look beyond simply "adding on" some aspects of different cultures and thinking of that as a successful form of multiculturalism/anti-racism. In essence, the book calls for us to move beyond the celebration of "Heroes and Holidays" (Lee, Menkart, and Okazawa-Rey 1998) and think critically about developing an integrated and inclusive curriculum that would empower our students. It also forces us to address what exactly our roles are as teachers.

If I were a teacher, I thought, when I have to teach about classical music I could also integrate Indian and Chinese classical music. When we have to look at jazz I could bring in so many variances of jazz from Africa. That would do more to empower my students in seeing their cultures also reflected in what they learnt (at least in my mind). It was as important as the other things they were learning and it would help them to develop a sense of pride in their culture and value their heritage.

Anti-discrimination pedagogy and the need for inclusive schooling does not intend to displace a Eurocentric view but it intends to decenter its position from appearing to be "the solely important and only valid perspective." By integrating other approaches, it shares its value among the many other forms of knowledge and makes them equally as valid.

As my class continued, it only felt worst for me. Not because the teacher was bad but [because] I felt horribly uncomfortable with the two activities that she chose for us. My mind flashed immediately to my first class in Physical Education and how uncomfortable I was in the first activity that we did in class. That time, I did not participate in the activity.

In music, my teacher asked us to all stand in a circle and do a song where we would end up holding hands with our partner. While holding hands may seem simple to so many, for Muslims and other groups especially from the sub-continent, cross-gender interaction is for many, minimal. Respect across the genders is shown by NOT having physical contact (unless you are directly related to the person).

I felt a horrible gulf in my stomach as I thought to myself, "Great, now you will have to sit out." "Here you go again being different." I wished more than anything that she said we did not need to hold hands and that the activity was modified. It only got worst. As we progressed, we were told to link arms with the other partner and move around to a new partner. My fist partner was male and I was totally comfortable but when we had the "surprise" that we moved to a new partner, I felt very uncomfortable because then it was a female. Somewhere in the back of my mind I thought about the students in my school again and how uncomfortable some of them would be. So I quickly turned to my partner and I told her I was quite uncomfortable for religious reasons and she helped to modify it so there was no physical contact between us BUT we both participated and still had fun.

Later on we would have to not only link arms and move but we would have to hit each other with our hips on both sides. The class I so looked forward to rapidly made me feel very uncomfortable. I resolved to e-mail my teacher and let her know.

Removing the Margins also talked about empowering students based on their own "social location." That involved knowing the community the student came from and including the parent of the child in knowing and understanding how to handle such situations. The community is looked at as being an untapped source of knowledge that can help to strengthen the classroom. Bringing parents and community members into the classroom only serves to enrich the curriculum that is being taught to the students and ensures that they see themselves reflected in a positive manner. It also serves the function of teaching the students how to look at the same issues with different perspectives, something that is important in a pluralistic community and within the wider context of a "global village."

As teachers, we are all influenced by our own identities, histories, and beliefs (Freire 1968). It is critical that we continually ask ourselves to evaluate and reflect on how we approach issues of anti-racism within our own classrooms. As I mentioned before, when students are marginalized they disengage themselves from the system and can quickly find themselves either in trouble (academically or socially) or they may drop out (or rather get "pushed out") of school altogether.

I may not have all the answers now, but I plan to do the best that I can to empower my students through their learning. In the meantime, I think I will talk to my teacher and let her know how I felt in class today. Every negative experience can always be changed to a positive one if we challenge ourselves and push ourselves to take that extra step. However, I do this with the realization that students don't always feel comfortable to approach their teachers with their feelings. It is of the utmost importance that we realize that as teachers we are in positions of power and [that] many times students may feel that they cannot approach us, especially when I considered how I felt in these situations and the fact that I felt uncomfortable and unable to say anything. What about young students who feel that they cannot challenge their teachers or that the only way to challenge them or get their attention is to act out? It made me even more cognizant of the fact that we need to work diligently as educators to ensure that we create a safe environment in our classrooms. This would ensure that our students see us as people who teach them and learn from them as well and that we value what we teach to them and value what we learn from them.

Semester 2, 2003

In every community there exists diversity in how we look at the world and our views and opinions about various issues. We all come with a perspective and view about reality, justice, injustice, and what is right and wrong amongst the myriad of variables that makes each of us an individual. Still, as a collective, we form a community, and these communities exist within our classrooms.

It is with this spirit in mind that I would like to reflect on some issues that made me uncomfortable or were exclusionary. I do not pretend to speak for or represent other voices. However, I think this discussion can be useful in creating a more constructive and thoughtful preservice course for teacher candidates and classroom teachers.

Firstly, I feel that not all preservice education classes are not reflective of the diversity that exists in the wider society. I know that there is a standard application process that all candidates must go through, but the fact that the classes are not more diverse tells me that there is a need to review the admissions process. Is there a predominance of any particular group of people? If so, why? How mixed are the classes (race, gender, socioeconomic status, class, etc.)? Do students in preservice see themselves reflected at this level? I think that these are important questions that need to be addressed at an institutional level in order to ensure that the admissions requirements are equitable and fair.

Another way that I think we can build on inclusion within our preservice classes is to look at the materials we use. This is something that has often been stressed. As a teacher it is important to try to make sure that my students feel that they are represented, that they are empowered from a variety of sources of information. This can be done through the literature I make available to my class, by the experts I choose to consult or bring into my classroom or use in projects, by the examples I bring into the class, and by the pictures and class work I have displayed in the classroom, among many other practical tools.

This becomes even more important when we think about educating our students to understand different points of view in their education, to understand that no one group of people has a monopoly on knowledge and learning. In fact, knowledge that exists today is the combined work, over time, of numerous groups of diverse people. Each one adds to the fabric of life and knowledge as we know it today. This allows our students to see themselves reflected in their education, allowing them to develop the awareness that it is possible for them to become owners of knowledge and that this can be attributed to and contributed to the world around them. The implications of this are that it would engage our students in their process of learning and also develop their critical thinking skills.

The other thing that I found is that sometimes in a bid to promote equity, we privilege certain forms of oppression over others. For example, in our research for our mini-seminars we covered a variety of issues, including homophobia. In fact, homophobia was covered again in our leadership sessions and then again by a professor at the end of the year. We do need to learn about oppression as it exists in its various forms. But the message that this sends to a class is that this IS oppression, this is what we consider to be important (to the exclusion of other forms of oppression).

In a post–September 11th environment, followed by the Iraqi war and the Intifada in Palestine, I would have to say that Islamophobia and anti-Semitism are important. Someone else in our class may think ableism is important, others may think classism is necessary to address. In fact, the latter became an issue when people in class were trying to promote certain activities such as the graduation and others could not afford it and felt excluded.

As this is applied to our classrooms, it is important for us to realize that we need to be even more careful as we may discuss one form of oppression and totally exclude other students who are dealing with totally different issues. This indirectly sends the message that we do not care, which is not what any teachers would want their students to think but what students may feel. Especially when we remember that we are in positions of power and students may not feel comfortable enough to approach us with these issues. "Why was it fair for some to address their positions or beliefs and not fair for others?" was often asked. We have opinions that can be equally shared within a framework of tolerance and respect, but what happens when students are not allowed to say anything?

Again, in our classroom management workshop done mid-year, one of the characteristics of a bad teacher again was homophobia (which is true).

This was written with a list of other characteristics that did not include many other negative discriminatory practices. My point here is that we cannot discuss one form of oppression and ignore others. As educators I think that we need to focus on these within a context of interlocking forms of oppression. We need to see, understand, and realize how different forms of oppression are interconnected and how they can impact on all students in the class.

Can we discuss or list all forms of oppression? Personally, I don't think so, but we also need to be careful in how we present information to our classes. We also need to be aware that if we list one form of oppression, then we need to solicit more or others from our class to make sure that we at least create an opportunity for students to feel included as well. We need to learn the skills that can facilitate disagreements but foster respect. I believe that this is possible.

Terminology and semantics are also important in how we deal with such issues and how people perceive their importance. In one of my classes, we had a rubric that asked us to do a self-evaluation of the way we were interacting in our class. One of the sections on the rubric was "interacting with others of diversity." When I read this, I thought to myself, "Who are these diverse people?" Did it mean minoritized students (a.k.a. visible minorities) or did it mean others who were different from us? This term was very vague and I thought about how students could/would have perceived it. In this case it could have been quite negative or varied and cause confusion in the minds of students.

Approaching equity is a sensitive issue and we need to be careful as we try to promote equity in one way that we are not indirectly promoting the opposite in another way. Another example of this occurred when we had a session on gender and equity in the classroom. After that discussion, many people left saying that they were going to make all these changes in their classes by mixing groups, in letting their students engage in gender-mixed activities. I personally believe that these are important aspects in the development of a child. However, if a child comes from a culture where he or she is socialized according to gender, if a teacher is not careful, this can be quite traumatic. I have seen female students break into tears when they were placed in groups with boys without proper groundwork being done by teachers. I have also seen boys who were very uncomfortable but reduced to silence instead of actively participating.

Many children who come from the subcontinent such as Hindus, Muslims, and Sikhs often socialize within gender-specific groups. The same can be said for many who have Middle Eastern and some African backgrounds.

What we include is also as important as what we exclude, and I think that it is really important to touch on issues around including diverse cultures within our practice. In another class, I sat as a teacher read a piece to the class that mentioned many of the thinkers, leaders, and religious figures through time—Confucius, Buddha, Moses, Jesus, and others. It leads me to an important question: Do we need to mention every group all the time? I don't think so, as long as we mention some of them some of the time and are able to get a holistic picture of different worldviews. This did not happen in my class and so I felt somewhat excluded even though I knew the instructor never intended for this to happen.

Often because there are no people to advocate for inclusion of these voices and the overwhelming workload that teachers may have, they may be excluded to everyone's detriment. I reemphasize the point that I do not believe that these things are intentional. They are a function of course structures, lack of time, lack of resources, overwhelming workloads that instructors have to deal with, and societal beliefs and values. However, it is still important and needs to be constantly addressed as it impacts students at so many levels.

This issue is quite complex and can appear to be quite daunting, but it should never prohibit us from continuing to push ourselves beyond our current levels of knowledge. One of the first things I learned from consultants such as Enid Lee and Marcela Duran when I was doing the anti-racism mini-seminar was that having or developing an anti-discrimination pedagogical approach is an ongoing task that never ends. So we keep learning and implementing strategies in the ways that we know until we learn or realize that we could be excluding others. My class provided me with an invaluable opportunity to grow and expand the horizons of my knowledge and to push the boundaries of my learning.

As teachers at every level, we need to use our classrooms as platforms to promote respect, equity, and tolerance. We will never have a classroom that has homogenous thinkers, so we need to move toward inclusive dialogue, accepting differing points of view, promoting respect and tolerance, and dismantling hatred in all of its forms. This is the only way, in my view, that we can promote, encourage and develop an inclusive and respectful society.

References

Dei, G. 2000. *Removing the Margins: The Challenges and Possibilities of Inclusive Schooling*. Toronto: Canadian Scholars' Press.

Freire, P. 1968. *Pedagogy of the Oppressed*. New York: Herder and Herder.

Henderson, A. T., C. L. Marburger, and T. Ooms. 1986. *Beyond the Bake Sale: An Educator's Guide to Working with Parents*. Columbia, Md.: National Committee for Citizens in Education.

Lee, E., D. Menkart, and M. Okazawa-Rey, eds. 1998. *Beyond Heroes and Holidays: A Practical Guide to K–12 Anti-Racist, Multicultural Education and Staff Development*. Washington, D.C.: Network of Educators on the Americas.

Issues of diversity and social stratification in the classroom and at school have been addressed in many ways. Perhaps a useful view of such issues is presented in the summary of the following article, which focuses on the necessity for educators to not only rethink their curricula but also to redefine their roles with respect to the students they teach and the varied and various communities that they serve.

ADDRESSING DIVERSITY AND
SOCIAL STRATIFICATION AT SCHOOL

In an article entitled "Empowering Minority Students: A Framework for Intervention," Cummins (2001) notes that over the past several decades, educators and politicians have implemented a series of costly but largely unsuccessful reforms, including compensatory programs, bilingual education programs, hiring of additional aides and remedial personnel, and the institution of safeguards against discrimination, aimed at reversing the pattern of school failure among marginalized, at-risk, disadvantaged, and minority students. Cummins suggests that the reason many of these programs fail is because relationships between teachers and students and between schools and communities have essentially remain unchanged. While legislative and policy reforms may be necessary conditions for effective change, they are insufficient measures because deep change involves redefinitions of the way in which educators interact with the students and communities they serve and within which they establish their influence.

Cummins proposes a theoretical framework for examining the types of personal and institutional redefinitions required to reverse the pattern of minority-student failures. This framework assigns a central role to power relations between teachers and students, schools and marginalized communities, and the intergroup relations within the society as a whole. The variability of at-risk students' educational achievements under differing social and educational conditions indicates that many complex, interrelated factors, including educational quality and cultural mismatch as well as status and power relations between groups, are at work. Each of the following dimensions represents a continuum that reflects the extent to which students are empowered or disabled as a direct result of their interactions with educators in the schools.

- The extent to which the language and culture of marginalized, at-risk, disadvantaged, and minority students are incorporated into existing school programs
- The extent to which the participation of marginalized, at-risk, disadvantaged, and minority communities is encouraged as an integral component of student education
- The extent to which the pedagogy promotes intrinsic motivation on the part of students to use language to actively generate their own knowledge
- The extent to which educators and other professionals advocate for students rather than legitimize the location of the problem in the students themselves

Widespread school failure does not occur in minority groups that are positively oriented toward both their own and the dominant culture, that do not perceive themselves as inferior to the dominant group, and that are not alienated from their own cultural values. While the dominant group controls institutions and reward systems within society, the *dominated* group is often exposed to conditions, such as limited access to economic and educational resources and ambivalence toward cultural transmission and primary language use and interaction styles that may not resemble interaction patterns in school, that predispose students to school failure. Furthermore, Cummins states that there is sufficient overlap in the impact of cognitive/academic and identity factors to justify incorporation of these two dimensions within the context of student empowerment while recognizing that under differing conditions, each dimension may be affected in different ways.

Even assessment can be seen as a crucial impediment to learning since many assessment tools are culturally biased, psychological or educational tests. Such assessment tools tend to locate the difficulty within marginalized, at-risk, disadvantaged, or minority students themselves, in effect screening them from deficits within the school program itself, the historical systemic elitist orientation of educators toward these students, and traditional transmission models of education that result in blaming students for their own lack of success. Issues such as these also inhibit students from developing active participation and contribute to a subsequent inability to develop critical approaches to their own learning and knowledge development.

Students may be disempowered by schools in much the same way as their communities are disempowered by societal institutions. Since equality of opportunity is seen as a given, individuals are often believed to be responsible for their own failure and are made to feel guilty, inferior, or both. These students will succeed educationally only to the extent that the patterns of interaction in school reverse those that prevail in the larger society. In short, Cummins suggests that, in the absence of definitions of the roles of individual educators and educators as a group, schools will continue to reproduce the power relations that characterize the wider society. This will, in turn, jeopardize success in schooling and in the wider society for marginalized, at-risk, disadvantaged, and minority students. In order to reverse this pattern of widespread replication of dominant culture values, educators may wish to ensure that their educational policies, practices, and procedures will encourage students and teachers to become critical thinkers capable of transforming society for positive social change.

IMPLICATIONS FOR THE CLASSROOM

Contradictions between the rhetoric of equality and the reality of domination may be exposed and dealt with through the lens of critical inquiry. Tension, nervousness, and fear may be some of the emotions that can be anticipated when topics that probe the nature of diversity and social stratification are engaged, simply because students' lives are under scrutiny. They may feel violated, disadvantaged, or even guilty for subscribing to the societal strata or the ethnicity into which they were born. However, overall, it is better to talk about it, explore it, and engage with it, than to pretend that equality and equity are givens. Some unpleasantness may be inevitable, but from engagement with these issues, a greater understanding and tolerance, if not acceptance, may emerge. Following is a short list (which is by no means exhaustive) of caveats for discussions around matters of diversity and social stratification.

In order to deal with diversity and social stratification in the classroom:

- Talk about it, but don't dwell on it. Students like to be seen as people, not just as members of a disadvantaged (or advantaged) group.
- Information is crucial. One method of providing information that is more effective than preaching is to have students get to know one another.
- Try to be as positive as possible. Making people feel guilty is usually not successful.
- Allow for a degree of self-interest and "inner group" orientation. These are natural and valuable human qualities.
- Encourage students to understand that we can be proud of our race, culture, nation, status in society, education, and wealth (or the lack thereof) without seeing it as superior.
- Building community in the classroom through the development of a safe learning environment can be a basis for reducing prejudice and discrimination. An effective community promotes knowledge of others, motivation to change, and intergroup skills.
- Modeling by the teacher is extremely important. A main teaching against bias will occur through modeling. People sense immediately whether teachers are accepting or biased. Teachers may work on their own perspectives through reading, traveling, getting to know individu-

als from walks of life different from their own, and through discussions, to mention just a few methods.

- The three different issues of stereotyping, prejudice, and discrimination must each receive attention.
- While affirmative action may be necessary, if it is poorly implemented, it can make matters worse.
- Be wary of people who dismiss emphasis on issues of diversity and social stratification as mere political correctness. Speaking and behaving in an unbiased way is important.

In matters of differing equity among students, it is important to bear in mind that neither equity nor equality are distributed democratically. For example, English-as-a-second-language learners suffer from the same range and frequency of learning differences as do native-born learners. However, in the case of second-language learners, while learning differences often interfere with the learning of the language, it is more difficult to sort language issues from learning issues. Educators can benefit from understanding that vulnerabilities in language skills are intensified for second-language learners, especially those with learning differences, because those students are not only trying to learn new information in a variety of subjects in a new language, they are trying to learn a new language as well. As a result, it is important for educators to continue to inform themselves about new research on educational issues and to ensure that the classroom environment promotes success in learning by striving to meet the needs of the individual learners and to adopt teaching strategies that are fair to all cultures. This classroom environment may feature a reciprocal interaction model of pedagogy that allows students the freedom to generate, create, and develop their own forms of knowledge and expression. The use of this model, which incorporates the central tenet of talking and writing as a means to learning, requires a genuine dialogue between educator and student in oral and written work. It requires guidance and facilitation and the encouragement of student-to-student talk in a collaborative learning context. Such a model emphasizes the development of the higher-level cognitive skills that are a hallmark of critical thinking. In this model, language use and development are consciously integrated with all curricular content rather than taught as isolated subjects, and tasks are presented to students in ways that generate intrinsic rather than extrinsic motivation (Cummins 2001).

Following is a list of possible teaching and instructional techniques that may be useful in assisting students who are at risk:

- Allow wait time for students to answer questions and complete in-class and homework assignments and tests.
- Consider administering tests in alternative formats such as orally or by computer.
- Whenever appropriate, present material using graphic and/or sensory media.
- Combine both auditory and visual stimuli—say it *and* write it.
- Word processors may be used whenever possible, as this makes rewriting and revising much less difficult.
- Make it easy for students to ask for repetition. Bear in mind that it may be important to use the same words when you do repeat so that you do not change the construct and defeat the purpose of the repetition. Also, differentiate between repetition and the explanation of a concept in a different way.
- Do not give too many instructions at one time. Break tasks into component parts and issue instructions for each part separately.
- Allow reading in advance for students to think about items to be covered in class. Provide plenty of pre-discussion, pre-writing, pre-reading, and other pre-teaching strategies.
- Plan lessons to explicitly state the topic and progress from the obvious to the concrete to the abstract. Try not to jump without warning from one topic to another.
- Frame material by relating it to past classroom or personal experience and by highlighting new material.
- Whenever possible, group material so that it is organized by category.
- Take notes on how students think they learn best and what issues are relevant to them.
- Look for students' balancing strengths and recognize, praise, and reinforce areas of competence wherever possible.
- Active knowledge generation can occur when students create and publish their own books and newspapers within the classroom or school environment.

It may be noticed that many of these suggestions are simply good teaching practices that may benefit *all* students. While it may be impossible to close the gap between students who are marginalized, at risk, or disadvantaged and those students who represent the social elite, educators may lessen the effects of social stratification through the incorporation of practices, processes, and procedures aimed at promoting equity through fair and equitable teaching strategies and by encouraging discussion and examination of social justice issues through critical inquiry. Use other strategies for course adaptation wherever possible to accommodate learners who are experiencing difficulty with the various biases of the curriculum, including reducing the syllabus to essential details, slowing the pace of instruction, reducing the vocabulary demands, providing continuous review, and incorporating visual/tactile/kinesthetic (multisensory) stimulation and support. Classroom teachers and other educators may also use cooperative learning strategies, positive reinforcement, physical activities, and visual aids across curriculum topics.

SUPPORTING STUDENTS TO BECOME ACTIVE GENERATORS

The following list represents possibilities that may assist and support the incorporation of nondominant cultures into the school program. It consists of supportive strategies for students to become active in generating their own knowledge. Language is considered to be central to the understanding of learning processes as well as to the understanding of the process of learning to think critically.

- Represent the various cultural groups in the school and district by providing signs in the administrative office and elsewhere that welcome people in their own language, by providing multilingual signs, and by incorporating greetings and information in various languages in newsletters and other school communications.
- Encourage students to use their preferred language at school (when English is not being used in the classroom as a medium of instruction) and provide resources, such as tutors and library resources, for students from nondominant cultures.

- Welcome pictures and objects of various cultures into the curriculum and provide opportunities for students to study their first language in elective subjects or in extracurricular clubs.
- Encourage parents to assist in the classroom, library, and clubs and invite people from all walks of life to act as resource people and to be part of a speakers' bureau for both formal and informal settings.
- Use split texts with English on one page and the language of choice on the facing page.
- Genuine dialogue is essential between student and teacher in all educational modalities. This may mean the encouragement of meaningful language rather than merely the correctness of surface forms.
- Educators may wish to guide and facilitate student development rather than attempt to control learning. This could serve to encourage student-to-student talk in a collaborative and safe learning and teaching environment.
- Foster a sense of critical inquiry through a focus on higher-order learning skills rather than merely concentrating on factual recall.
- Present student work that generates intrinsic rather than extrinsic motivation. Involve students in curriculum planning, teaching, and learning and developing an awareness of students' various learning styles (Cummins 1991).

All too often, the instruction that is received by minority groups or students who are at risk within the larger society convinces them that their point of view is either irrelevant, inaccurate, or incorrect. Subsequent failures are then taken as an indication that the student is terminally unmotivated, intellectually compromised, or both. In order to support students to become more active and assertive in generating their own knowledge, the teacher can assist by becoming more aware of issues that are relevant to students' lives. It is these lived experiences that will provide the material for the development of their own ways of seeing and being in the world.

CONCLUSION

The total effect of this chapter may be to raise more questions than it answers, but raising questions in a critical environment is important to the eventual understanding of complex, competing, and integrated issues. And so it is with issues of diversity and social stratification. While these two issues have frequently been considered separately, it is equally important to view them as obverse and converse sides of the same perspective by situating diversity within the context of a socially stratified society.

In attempts to position diversity within the vicissitudes of the larger society, it becomes challenging to tease specific issues out from the larger context in order to further understand how they act and are acted upon. It may be the case, as well, that a diverse student body is diverse in a multiplicity of ways or that individual students may suffer as a result of being at risk, subscribing to a visible minority, and being marginalized all at the same time. In short, it may be no surprise that disadvantaged students often suffer from multiple "disadvantages" as defined and sustained by society within the school and beyond. Conversely, the upper end of the social stratification continuum, the so-called elite, are often elite in many ways, since they usually have a multiplicity of advantages to choose from simply by having greater access to financial, educational, social, and cultural capital, to identify only a few.

Needless to say, diversity is valuable. It can provide a mirror by which the society can view itself. The way that diverse populations are treated within schools and society can be powerful indications of the societal values. It should be a matter of pride and a belief in the intrinsic goodness of society to benefit all of its members regardless of their position on the continuum of social strata. Social stratification is an artificial barrier to equity that, once recognized and challenged, can result in benefits for everyone within society, regardless of whether they are marginalized, disadvantaged, exceptional in some way, or at risk or subscribe to a visible minority.

Unfortunately, it must be emphasized that teaching is an essentially middle-class, dominant culture–oriented activity and well-meaning individuals may benefit from the development of a deeper, stronger, and more wide-ranging critical lens in order to challenge a socioeducational system that tends to systematically disable large segments of the population.

The following chapter promises to take this analysis a step farther by attempting to isolate and expand understanding surrounding anti-discrimination education.

IDEAS FOR STUDY

1. Discrimination is often more than a single incident. The template in Supplementary Material focuses on daily practices that help to identify included and excluded individuals and groups of people. Discuss the items on the list and feel free to add other items. If answers to any of these questions are negative, you may be able to identify areas that require work in your school or classroom.

2. There are many obstacles to the task of overcoming poverty in Western society. Some individuals, however, do manage to become successful despite the odds. Are there common patterns found in the stories of these individuals? You may either research and share a family story of such an individual or research the life of a famous person who came from poverty.

   How does that person define success? What factors enabled that individual to succeed? In what ways was formal education enabling or disabling?

3. Bring to class teaching resources that promote the idea of a society in which you would like to live. The resource may be as simple as a children's book or a newspaper article. Be prepared to justify your choice.

4. If you could interview one individual who could add a fresh or enlightened perspective to our dialogue on social stratification and discriminatory practices, who would that be and why?

5. What sorts of examples of class disparities or discriminatory practices in schooling did you see in your practice teaching? As a prospective thoughtful teacher, can you think of a constructive way to rewrite this experience?

6. Find statements from your institution or school board that illustrate policies relating to diversity and social stratification. Are these policies informative and is it possible to implement them successfully?

SUPPLEMENTARY MATERIAL: DIVERSITY AND SOCIAL STRATIFICATION QUESTIONNAIRE

1. Does the school communicate effectively between home and school in terms of inclusive practices?

2. Have you been taught how to detect bias in your study materials and teaching resources?
3. Do students of similar backgrounds seem to stick together in class, on teams, at lunch, and in other areas and activities within the school or classroom?
4. Does the material you study or teach include authors from a variety of backgrounds, and do courses stress the contributions of all cultural and racial groups?
5. Are parents viewed as rich resources for promoting the celebration of all contributing cultures and walks of life?
6. Do all school personnel take situations seriously in which discrimination regarding race or class may play a part?
7. Are all students and teachers treated fairly and equitably, or are some students and/or teachers favoured over others based on class and/or race?

REFERENCES

Cummins, J. 2001. Empowering minority students: A framework for intervention. In *An Introductory Reader to the Writings of Jim Cummins*, ed. C. Baker and N.H. Homberger. Clevedon, England: Multilingual Matters.

Cummins, J. 1991. Empowering culturally and linguistically diverse students with learning problems. Reston, Va.: ERIC Clearinghouse on Handicapped and Gifted Children.

Edelsky, C., ed. 1999. *Making Justice Our Project: Teachers Working toward Critical Whole Language Practice*. Urbana, Ill.: National Council of Teachers of English.

Hale, J. 1994. *The Old Way of Seeing*. New York: Houghton Mifflin.

Kymlicka, W. 2000. Comment: An ethnic stitch in time. *The Globe and Mail* (Toronto), December 27, A15.

RECOMMENDED READING

Brice, A., and C. McKibbin. 1999. Turning frustration into success for English language learners. *Educational Leadership* 56, no. 7 (April): 53–55.

Cummins, J. 2001. *Language, Power, and Pedagogy: Bilingual Children in the Crossfire*. Clevedon, England: Multicultural Matters.

Edwards, B. 1989. *Drawing on the Right Side of the Brain*. Los Angeles: Jeremy P. Tarcher Inc.

Gardner, H. 1993. *Multiple Intelligences: The Theory in Practice*. New York: Basic Books.

Chapter Eight

Anti-Discrimination Education

People do have innate standards, but most do not know how to get at them. It is hard for people to separate the important from the unimportant.

—Hale (1994, 25)

Some people prefer the term "anti-racist education" to "multicultural education," believing that these terms are interchangeable. However, we believe that this is a mistaken assumption and prefer to think of anti-racism and multiculturalism as two perspectives on the same issue. Anti-racism deals with the recognition of stereotyping, prejudice, and discrimination and attempts to eradicate such maladjustments through positive actions aimed at improving social justice for all. It is for this reason that the term "anti-discrimination education" is used throughout this chapter

Stereotyping is the real-life equivalent of poetic metonymy, in which a part represents a whole. Stereotyping is reductionist, however, in that it allows an entire race or culture to be reduced to a single set of (generally reprehensible) characteristics. Through stereotyping, entire groups of individuals are scapegoated and punished by other individuals or a populace who choose to believe that the targeted group can be viewed in terms of one or two (generally negative) characteristics. Much of the target groups' subscription to identity is called into question and broad assumptions about individual characteristics within the group are transferred to the whole group. This, of course, is unfair. Even if the characteristics that are used to stand for the entire population of the target group are positive characteristics, it still diminishes the group by reducing their capacities significantly and ignoring the diversity among individuals within the group.

Prejudice and discrimination all too frequently follow on the heels of stereotyping. Prejudice is the harbouring of inaccurate attitudes and perceptions about individuals or groups of individuals and is most often based on external characteristics such as physiognomy, cultural mannerisms or clothing, food, and accent. Other significant traits that frequently become currency in the production of prejudice are religion, race, and attitudes held by the target group, often a minority population held in a position of relative powerlessness. It is often difficult or even impossible to change the way one thinks about individuals or a group of individuals based on physical differences, appearances, or cultural mannerisms. In fact, it has been claimed that we all have some form of prejudice, and while this may be true, it is impossible to eradicate prejudice without limiting one's ability to discern quality. If prejudice cannot be eliminated, it is necessary to *not* act upon prejudices, to question our assumptions about our own and others' beliefs, and to educate ourselves about the causes of stereotyping, prejudice, and discrimination.

Discrimination is the acting out of prejudice and is harmful to both the perpetrator and the victim, much the same way that bullying harms both victim and bully. The three focal points of inappropriate attitudes, beliefs, and actions all function through fear of the unknown. In this case, fear of the unknown is generated by the deliberate or unintentional misunderstanding of another individual's or group's way of being in the world.

Multiculturalism represents a much more positive response to issues of diversity. While multiculturalism has been recently criticized as being shallow because it addresses superficial aspects of diversity such as the "4 Ds" (dance, dinner, dialect, and dress), it can be used to celebrate similarities among cultures rather than differences between them. As the opposite side of the diversity coin, multicultural practices, policies, and procedures can help to supplement, amplify, and reinforce those strategies aimed at reducing and eliminating racism in schools and ultimately in the larger society.

Race and cultural differences need to be acknowledged in order to provide a safe and nurturing learning environment. Curricular materials may encourage students to critically evaluate and examine negative and dismissive images of stereotypical caricatures encountered through their educational and social processes.

ESL STUDENTS WITH LEARNING DISABILITIES

Many educators may be unaware that second-language learners suffer from the same rate, range, and severity of learning differences as do first-language learners. In her burning issue essay, Anh Hoang writes about how ESL students with learning differences are currently being diagnosed. Diagnosis is particularly difficult because a learning difference may be subtle enough to remain undetected as a result of students' compensatory strategies. This article also addresses ways of identifying students with learning differences and some of the obstacles faced by educators that make it difficult to identify and diagnose these students.

Reasons for Choice of Topic

Through many years of teaching ESL, I have found myself wondering from time to time whether there is a possibility that some students might have a learning disability that is blocking their progress in learning English. As an ESL student myself, I have experienced the challenges of learning a second language, but is it really the anxiety of being afraid to make mistakes in grammar or pronunciation that is the cause of the failure? Is it possible that many of the ESL students who are considered to be "poor language learners" are struggling simply because they also have a learning disability? Through my personal and volunteer experiences I have noticed that in many countries/cultures, learning disabilities are not recognized, or in some cases they are recognized by the teachers but ignored by the parents or institutions. In my second-language acquisition class I have done some research on second-language learners and learning disabilities and found some interesting figures and helpful hints. In this research project, I would like to critically examine the topic of learning disabilities (learning issues, learning differences, and learning problems) in conjunction with ESL students. I hope that from this learning investigation I will learn more about the painful collision of ESL and LD and come up with some strategies that I can incorporate into the curriculum to improve the classroom environment for all students.

Problem Addressed

- How can I as a teacher tell if an ESL student is learning disabled?
- How, when, to what extent can I do something as a teacher to accommodate their needs?
- Are there special programs, special aides, or teaching strategies to help ESL-LD students in regular classrooms?

Summary of Research Findings and Personal Insights

Introduction

Research shows that awareness of learning disabilities (LD) is an increasingly prominent issue in education, yet this fact has been widely ignored in the ESL classroom and in schools in general until very recently. It is possible that many of the ESL students who are considered to be poor language learners are struggling because they also have a learning disability. This essay investigates what is known about ESL learners and learning disabilities, suggests ways to identify ESL students who may have learning disabilities, and gives teachers/educators strategies to incorporate into the curriculum to improve the classroom environment for all students.

Difficulties in Identifying ESL Students with Learning Disabilities

ESL learners may show learning disabilities in a second language when they do not do so in their first language. A learning disability may also be so subtle in a first language that it is masked by an individual's compensatory strategies. For example, students with learning difficulties may be able to get general information through the overall context when specific words or concepts are not understood and by substituting known words for words they do not understand. These strategies may not be available to the learner in the second language (Ganschow and Sparks 1993). Other reasons for difficulties in identifying LD in ESL learners may be that the field of second-language acquisition has historically blamed language-learning failure on a number of factors other than learning disability. The factors cited in the language-learning literature have been lack of effort, lack of motivation, poor language-learning habits, and anxiety about language learning. Among other causes, anxiety in the foreign language classroom (anxiety about making mistakes in grammar and pronunciation, about understanding the teacher's instruction, about remembering vocabulary) has been prominent as an alleged cause of the failure.

Identifying Learning Disabled ESL Students
Common behaviours of ESL-LD students include lack of concentration and poor learning behaviours (constant fidgeting, not knowing what is going on in class, not completing work, and handing in incomplete or late assignments). It is true that these poor learning behaviours are common in all students and that such students are often considered by teachers to be simply unfocused or even lazy. Other methods of identifying learning disabilities such as standardized testing present many problems. The instruments designed to test learning disabilities are usually geared toward native English speakers; therefore, the results cannot be reliably used to test learners whose first language is not English. Also, the concepts and language being tested may have no direct translation; thus the validity of tests translated into the native language is questionable. Because no single assessment technique is sufficient to diagnose a learning disability at present, multiple assessment measures are necessary.

The Effect of Labeling ESL Students as Learning Disabled (Broader Issues)
Being identified/labeled as "learning disabled" can be stigmatizing for anyone—children, native English speakers, ESL students, and adult learners alike. Labeling a student as learning disabled can have a negative effect on his/her life emotionally and socially at home and school. Some cultures do not understand or recognize learning disabilities for what they are and thus may blame the culture itself or the student. Once the student is identified, the label and the accompanying stigma stays with him/her for a long period of time and this may have a significant

effect on his/her education and lifestyle. Therefore, before testing and labeling an ESL student (or any student for that matter) as learning disabled, teachers and parents must consider the level of severity and weigh the advantages of identifying the learner as learning disabled (planning special instruction to help the student, making him/her eligible for services/accommodations, etc.) against the possible negative stigma of the label.

Helpful Suggestions for Teachers, Students and Parents
Schools and universities who advertise their accommodation for learning disabled and other handicapped students may not recognize the LD-ESL collision problem. Students and families who ask schools for accommodation on this issue need to be well informed themselves and prepared to provide documentation or at least reference letters that will inform the school of this problem. More important, when possible, parents of young students or adult students should discuss the problem with a school before enrolling to be sure that their needs are accommodated. Again, as with all things associated with learning disabilities, the answers are often complex and long term, and every student's problem and solution is likely to be different. What is most important is that the problem of second-language learning for the learning disabled be recognized for what it is and that the student be fairly and reasonably accommodated (Brice and McKibbin 1999).

Case Studies on LD-ESL Students and Ways to Help Them
Howard Gardner's work on multiple intelligences and the different ways that people learn, remember, perform, and understand is helpful in understanding and accommodating ESL-LD students. Gardner has identified seven human intelligences: linguistic, logical-math, spatial, musical, bodily-kinesthetic, interpersonal, and intrapersonal (Gardner 1993, 11–12). According to Gardner's research, the best way to teach special-needs students is to identify their unique intelligence/style of learning and adjust the instruction and program for each student accordingly. Betty Edwards's work on the roles that the left brain and the right brain play in our thinking, reasoning, and complex mental functions is also helpful in explaining the various learning difficulties. (Left-brain characteristics include verbal, analytic, symbolic, abstract, temporal, rational, digital, and

linear patterns of thought and behavior while the right-brain characteristics can be described as nonverbal, nontemporal, nonrational, spatial, intuitive, and holistic; Edwards 1989, 12). Teachers can improve the learning environment for those with a learning disability by planning tasks so that differing intelligences are called upon and by balancing the involvement required of each hemisphere of the brain.

Ganschow and Sparks formulated a theory that explained the problems and variations in foreign language acquisition. Ganschow and Sparks's Linguistic Coding Deficit Hypothesis states that difficulties with foreign language acquisition stem from deficiencies in one or more of these linguistic codes in the student's native language system (Ganschow and Sparks 1993). These deficiencies result in mild to extreme problems with specific oral and written aspects of language. Their belief is that most learners having difficulties with foreign language learning have problems with "phonological awareness." That means that they have trouble with the basic sound units of language, phonemes, and do not recognize or otherwise manipulate these basic units of sound efficiently. Consequently, the student may have difficulty with the actual perception and production of language necessary for basic comprehension, speaking, and spelling or with language comprehension, which may affect understanding and/or production of language on a broader scale. According to Sparks and Ganschow's theory, excellent language learners are strong in all three of the linguistic codes and, conversely, very poor language learners are weak in all three. These difficulties spring from deficits in the native language. Ganschow and Sparks theorized that to help ESL-LD students, the sound system of the target language must be very explicitly taught.

In studying ESL-LD students, Ganschow and Spark discovered that when they were taught phonological skills in one language, the students improved their phonological awareness in English also. This finding has led to a variation on the method of teaching phonology in the target language: teach the fundamentals of phonology in the student's native language before foreign language instruction begins. Essentially, students learn what language is and how its sounds and parts function. Ganschow and Spark feel that students' reading and language skills will be much stronger and that future problems with foreign language acquisition will be fewer if such phonological skills are used early in a child's life.

Personal Insights and Conclusion

In my volunteer experiences and during my practicums I noticed that the number of ESL and LD students in schools has increased dramatically over the years. School districts are faced with the demanding task of preparing these ESL students to keep up academically with their native-English-speaking peers. Both of my practice teaching placements were in inner-city schools where there were many students whose first language is not English; some were identified as having learning difficulties, but many others showed signs of having difficulties but have not yet been identified. There is still little understanding of the fact that it is not a matter of having students with learning difficulties repeat a class or do an activity over again; it is a matter of recognizing and having them do it differently or do it at a later time. Teachers must understand that vulnerabilities in language skills are intensified for ESL students, especially those with learning disabilities, because those students are trying to learn not only new information in all subjects but also a new language. Therefore, teachers/educators must be informed about new research on educational issues and strive to ensure that the classroom environment does not perpetuate learning failure by limiting ESL-LD students' individual needs.

BIBLIOGRAPHY

Brice, A., and C. McKibbin. 1999. Turning frustration into success for English language learners. *Educational Leadership* 56, no. 7 (April): 53–55.

Edwards, B. 1989. *Drawing on the Right Side of the Brain*. Los Angeles, Calif.: Jeremy P. Tarcher, Inc.

Ganschow, Leonore, and Richard Sparks. 1995. Effects of direct instruction in Spanish phonology on the native language skills and foreign language aptitude of at-risk foreign language learners. *Journal of Learning Disabilities* 28, no. 2 (February): 107–120.

Ganschow, Leonore, and Richard Sparks. 1993. The impact of native language learning problems on foreign language learning: Case study illustrations of the linguistic coding deficit hypothesis. *Modern Language Journal* 77, no. 1: 58–74.

Gardner, H. 1993. *Multiple Intelligences: The Theory in Practice*. New York: Basic Books, Inc.

Learning Disabilities website: http://www.oise.utoronto.ca/-southopt/EP-Resources/Learning Disabilities.html.

It is all too unfortunate that the results of schooling occasionally conspire to effect a profound lack of belonging. Racial and cultural challenges make it all the more critical that educators understand how to make schools more hospitable and safe places for all students. As educators, we cannot ignore the needs of students to understand issues that are valuable, significant, and important to them and, by extension, to all of us.

ADDRESSING MULTICULTURALISM AND ANTI-RACISM AT SCHOOL

Self-knowledge alone is an insufficient base for teachers in today's society—a society that is, in general, widely diverse. Teachers—especially those of Eurocentric backgrounds—are often culturally, experientially, and linguistically disadvantaged when it comes to teaching students from a wide variety of backgrounds. Cultural knowledge from nondominant perspectives, relevant curricula, and effective instructional strategies are required to supplement and extend the self-knowledge of educators teaching in cross-cultural environments.

Understanding of a variety of cultures is a high priority for many teachers today. However, many classrooms continue to reflect or are dominated by one particular culture. When there is little diversity in their school or community, what can teachers do? Selecting multicultural books for inclusion and focus within the classroom may help students understand and recognize contributions from all cultures. Because of its narrative and descriptive nature, literature invites students into sociocultural contexts as sympathetic listeners or sharers where issues of racism, discrimination, and inequity are made concrete. Multicultural literature may be used as a means for developing a cross-cultural dialogue (MacPhee 1997). Using multicultural literature from a transformational approach can help to bring content about marginalized groups to the centre of the curriculum. This approach is rooted in both fictitious and historical accounts of the struggles of marginalized individuals or groups, which provide factual information and establish a context for the specificity of individual actions. One of the major benefits of the transformational approach can be the development of critical-thinking skills and the inclusion of various perspectives regarding anti-discrimination education. While this journey may jar the senses, it is a necessary journey if teachers and students wish to address the systemic injustices "embedded within the very fabric of our society, hidden within our own subconsciousness" (MacPhee 1997).

It is important for teachers to encourage student learning about both individuated and systemic racism, both in terms of how it affects everyone and how it is experienced by the minority group. It is important that students develop strategies to confront such forms of racism and develop skills to successfully bring about positive social change. Not only can teachers assist their students in a critique of white supremacy, teachers themselves may wish to engage in such critiques as well. For decades, however, children's literature, for example, has focused on white Eurocentric characters. In fact McGee-Banks and Banks (1995) suggest that previously unrecognized groups may benefit from receiving "unequal focus time" during classroom discussions if equal representation is to be valued.

Often, whatever is white is considered to be the norm by which everything else is judged. Anti-discrimination education helps to move the Eurocentric perspective over to make room for other perspectives to be included. It is necessary for educators to distinguish between prejudice and privilege as white students are often accorded greater privileges over their nonwhite counterparts, both in school and society. Good teachers recognize diversity and seek to redress issues of prejudice and privilege in their classes by using a range of teaching methods and strategies to address cultural, religious, and language differences as well as societal and familial aspects of inequity. An equitable and respectful educator attempts to connect the students' lived experiences with relevant social issues in order to question issues of prejudice and privilege.

Both Sheets (2000) and Howard (2000) raise concerns about the white movement in multicultural education. While both authors represent opposite poles in this debate, four assumptions provide ample grounds for discussion:

- There *is* a "white movement" in multicultural education.
- Attention to the role of whites in multicultural education is a recent phenomenon.
- The growing body of literature on issues of whiteness is evidence of a resurgence of white supremacy and racism within multicultural education.
- The current focus on white identity development in multicultural education signals a shift away from equity pedagogy.

Teachers may also wish to question their own values and beliefs. They may benefit from developing a feeling of confidence and comfort with encountering conflict around the questions, concerns, and comments that arise as a result of the inclusion of anti-discrimination strategies. Teacher and student interaction is important, and emphasis must be placed on the inclusion of all students. The objective of inclusive strategies of anti-discrimination education is to develop a proactive attitude within the students and teacher in order for them to become agents of positive social change.

Educators may benefit from committing themselves to strategies that are at once self-reflective and self-critical about how educators make meaning of cultural and racial differences. The current system of whiteness serves to advantage some students while marginalizing others. Unfortunately, students of colour are often caught between broadening the enrollment base in educational institutions and the realities of their daily experiences in those institutions. In short, they are expected to be both coloured and noncoloured at the same time. Furthermore, students of colour carry the additional burden of attempting to teach peers and teachers about issues of diversity, multiculturalism, and racism, even though these students are in the process of learning about themselves and their position with respect to these issues. What is required is an exemplary teaching-learning process that encourages open and honest dialogue, critical thinking, and cooperative learning experiences in which whiteness can be deconstructed and dismantled within a context of anti-discrimination education.

By the same token, educators of colour may not have the same multi-cultural perspective or be representatives for their race, gender, or class and, in fact, may not be monolithic in their views but may traverse the spectrum, individually and in groups, of being multivocal or silent. Educators of colour, however, often find themselves outside of the dominant discourse of education.

ANTI-DISCRIMINATION EDUCATION

Anti-discrimination education emerges from an understanding that racism exists in society. Therefore, because school is a societal institution, it, too, is influenced by racism. Current educational curriculum, teaching, and institutions tend toward a cultural bias that is exclusionary and racist. Anti-discrimination education is able to cut across all curriculum areas and addresses the histories and lived experiences of those who have been marginalized and silenced. Its purpose is to help deal equitably with all cultural and racial difference that we find in the human family (Lee 1985). Educators may wish to continue to engage in professional development around these and all topics concerning issues of social justice. The aim of anti-discrimination education is the eradication of racism in all its various iterations. Its inclusive perspective permeates all subject areas and school practices. Anti-discrimination education attempts to equip teachers and students, collectively and individually, with the analytic tools required to critically examine the origins of racist ideas and practices and understand the implications of such practices through revealing the relationship between our own prejudices and the systematic discrimination practiced by institutions on a daily basis. Four stages are commonly identified in anti-discrimination education change processes:

Superficial. People incorporate cultural ceremonies, celebrations, and rituals into the school culture. Welcoming signs in a variety of languages may be part of the school's attempts to be inclusive.

Transitional. Units of study typically characterize a variety of cultures selected for study. These are separate units added to the main curriculum, which remains intact.

Structural. Units of study are integrated with existing units to provide an interdisciplinary approach to the study of anti-discrimination education. Critical questions such as "In whose interests are these units being studied?" or "Why do certain kinds of knowledge get hidden?" are asked as the centre of the curriculum begins to change to reflect inclusion of multiple cultural perspectives.

Social. Curriculum is interwoven with multicultural and anti-discrimination strategies, helping to promote positive social change in the larger community outside of school. Anti-discrimination education is used to empower people and to change their lives.

Anti-discrimination education also attempts to reveal and make transparent the structures in society that have helped to organize peoples' lives and institutions that limit some people on the basis of race while privileging others, again on the basis of race, pointing to the social ordering of people and groups as one of the major sources of racist ideas. Such an education explores how political, social, and economic paradigms reinforce and shape lives through daily exposure through the media, textbooks, and entertainment, to mention only a few. Also, anti-discrimination education attempts to expose inadequate explanations for peoples' different positions in society, such as the ethic that implies that all you need for success is hard work. Such education highlights some of the human-made social structures and barriers that limit individuals and groups from improving their chances in life, despite their best efforts.

Anti-discrimination education attempts to move society toward the construction of a true multicultural society by attempting to move beyond the superficial comfort level of cultures to examine deeper and more controversial issues and dimensions of culture that lead to positive social change.

Thomas (1984) describes the principles of anti-discrimination education:

- Information alone about other cultures will not increase tolerance or acceptance of these cultures.
- Culture is more than the study of how people live but considers their lived experiences and the circumstances in which they find themselves.
- Equal access to jobs, programs, and services is not as simple as it sounds because of the inherent principle of competition in the marketplace, including competing against others who may also require equal access.

- Anti-discrimination education attempts to engage both those who experience racism and those who are members of the dominant culture.
- Racism can only be challenged through informed, collective action.

Racism is learned and therefore can be unlearned. Changes may be made within the existing educational institutions to begin to benefit *all* students through the inclusion of multiple perspectives and experiences of minority or nondominant groups and through the development of a curriculum that is flexible enough to accommodate a variety of perspectives.

IMPLICATIONS FOR CLASSROOM PRACTICE

There have always been people who have fought against racism and social injustice. It is in the best interests of society to recognize how things truly are, and if we ignore the fact that some people benefit from racial injustice, we are not being honest with ourselves or others. It is impossible to have a genuine anti-discrimination stance without having a sense of critical inquiry. It is part of the responsibility of the teacher to assist students in questioning the society in which they live.

Curricula and strategies of teaching and learning that minimize or eliminate systemic discrimination are urgently required. Policy models and sanctions from central board offices may not be enough to expose racism in all its forms.

What does systemic racism look like in schools? Enid Lee (1985) suggests that it can occur when teachers unintentionally:

- Have low expectations of students from minority or culturally nondominant backgrounds
- Teach to low expectations, thus further disabling and marginalizing students from minority or culturally nondominant backgrounds
- Encourage students to accept a limited vision of themselves and behave accordingly
- Stream students into a particular subject area because they seem good at it while denying them the opportunity to develop in other important areas
- Forget to include or omit student experiences from the curriculum or fail to treat these experiences seriously in the classroom

For example, even a kindergarten class with children of different backgrounds is still fundamentally a monocultural environment if the toys and games that are available reflect only the dominant culture, race, and language. This extends to all classrooms and to all classroom strategies, from what kind of pictures are on the walls and what festivals are celebrated to how students are grouped and what kinds of interactions are deemed acceptable.

One valuable strategy is to develop a critical approach to uncover the bias in fiction and nonfiction alike. One way to do this is to look for the voice of people who have been frequently silenced, such as people of colour, poor people, people with disabilities, and so on. To have students move beyond the material in front of them and acknowledge people who have had cultural resources misappropriated from them, such as any number of musical genres, is to welcome a critical approach to teaching and learning.

Because literature is part of a historical and cultural milieu, it is representative of a wide variety of sociocultural attitudes and beliefs. Reading multicultural literature is one way that students may vicariously experience beliefs, attitudes, and values of culturally diverse individuals and groups. Children's multicultural literature can affirm and value students' own lived experiences from a transcultural perspective. Students may wish to develop their own stories and include their own illustrations—this strategy acknowledges that students are experts about their own lived experiences. This learning process validates student voices and may allow deeper inspection of lived experiences through the lens of what they perceive to be burning issues.

CONCLUSION

The process of educating ourselves and others about whiteness, racism, oppression, privilege, and how these concepts relate to education is not only about changing attitudes, improving relationships between people and becoming more sensitive to children. As Collins (1998) suggests, it is also about the participation of everyone—teachers, students, and parents—in the process of developing critical pedagogies and methods that challenge curricula, structures, and practices that privilege, support and validate existing elite individuals and groups of individuals. By providing students with the tools required to critically inquire into, examine, and evaluate inherent biases and prejudices that exist within society, educators may help to dismantle forms of inequality and discrimination for future generations.

In the final analysis, anti-discrimination education allows educators an opportunity to broaden and deepen the perspectives of the young people they teach and provide them with skills that ultimately may serve to create the tools necessary to effect positive social change. It is hoped that multicultural literature can act as a catalyst to encourage student dialogue about social issues, helping to encourage other's voices and whole selves to become critical inquirers and to eventually become agents for positive social change. Teachers and students can benefit from constantly engaging in a critical examination of their curriculum and their classroom policies, practices, and procedures. Teachers and students can engage others in developing a nonracist curriculum. They may also wish to develop an awareness of the impact of systemic racism in our daily lives, and they can develop tools to analyze the extent of racism and construct strategies that will affirm and validate the cultural experiences and identities of all students so that their voices will be heard, listened to, and heeded.

IDEAS FOR STUDY

1. Can white privilege exist in a classroom in the absence of a white teacher? Are you aware of any examples of white privilege in your school? Please describe what attempts have been made to deal with this.
2. In small groups, brainstorm a list of privileges that can be considered "white privilege." Report back to the larger group. Compare your lists to the one created by Peggy McIntosh listed under the Recommended Reading section.
3. Discuss ways in which literature, music, cultural artifacts, photographs, family trees, and other artifacts can be used to support the principles of equity and to embrace the uniqueness of every student.
4. Share and discuss practicum experiences that may have involved meeting the needs of students.

5. What is the difference between structural and systemic racism?
6. How may reflection be used to promote anti-discrimination education and the inclusion of all students?
7. Describe the difference between anti-racism and multiculturalism. Is it possible for one to exist without the other?
8. Discuss anti-discrimination strategies and how they could be incorporated into your classroom.
9. If multicultural education is about challenging the status quo and power differentials that serve to limit people, what administrative support would be beneficial?
10. Can anti-discrimination education occur in the absence of critical inquiry? Why or why not?
11. Find policy statements from your institution or school board that inform staff and students how to deal with incidents of racism. Do such policies provide information regarding how to deal with such incidents successfully?

REFERENCES

Collins, P. H. 1998. *Fighting Words: Black Women and the Search for Justice.* Minneapolis: University of Minnesota Press.

Hale, J. 1994. *The Old Way of Seeing.* New York: Houghton Mifflin.

Howard, G. R. 2000. Reflections on the "White movement" in multicultural education. *Educational Researcher* 29, no. 9 (December): 21–23.

Lee, E. 1985. *Letters to Marcia: A Teacher's Guide to Anti-Racist Education.* Toronto: Cross Cultural Communication Centre.

MacPhee, J. S. 1997. "That's not fair!": A White teacher reports on White first graders' responses to multicultural literature. *Language Arts* 74, no. 1 (January): 33–40.

McGee-Banks, C. A., and J. A. Banks. 1995. Equity pedagogy: An essential component of multicultural education. *Theory into Practice* 34, no. 3: 152–158.

Sheets, R. H. 2000. Advancing the field or taking center stage: The White movement in multicultural education. *Educational Researcher* 29, no. 9 (December): 15–21.

Thomas, B. 1984. Principles of anti-racist education. *Currents: Readings in Race Relations* 2, no. 3.: 20–24.

RECOMMENDED READING

Professional Resources

Coelho, E. 1998. *Teaching and Learning in Multicultural Schools: An Integrated Approach.* Clevedon, England: Multicultural Matters.

Dilg, M. A. 1999. *Race and Culture in the Classroom: Teaching and Learning through Multicultural Education.* New York: Teachers College Press.

Finazzo, D. 1997. *All for the Children: Multicultural Essentials of Literature.* Albany, N.Y.: Delmar Publishing.

Howard, G. 1999. *We Can't Teach What We Don't Know: White Teachers, Multiracial Schools.* New York: Teachers College Press.

McGee-Banks, C. A., and J. A. Banks. 1995. Equity pedagogy: An essential component of multicultural education. *Theory into Practice* 34, no. 3: 152–158.

McIntosh, P. 1990. White privilege: Unpacking the invisible knapsack. *Independent School* 49, no. 2 (Winter).

McIntyre, A. 1997. *Making Meaning of Whiteness: Exploring the Racial Identity of White Teachers.* Albany: SUNY Press.

Books That Promote Understanding

Baylor, B. 1986. *I'm in Charge of Celebrations.* New York: Charles Scribner's Sons.

Curtis, C. P. 1996. *The Watsons Go to Birmingham—1963.* New York: Delacourte.

Gregory, N. 1995. *How Smudge Came.* Red Deer, Alta.: Red Deer College Press.

Rylant, C. 1992. *Missing May.* New York: Orchard.

Part III

TOWARD A PEDAGOGY OF HOPE AND SCHOOL CHANGE

Small is the number of them that see with their own eyes and feel with their own hearts

— Albert Einstein (*Einstein: A Portrait*)

The intent of this book was and continues to be to provide individuals with opportunities for insight into the value and process of critical inquiry for both facilitating and exploring personal and professional relationships within the context of becoming teachers. This book examined how lived experiences reveal opportunities in which critical inquiry challenges teachers and their students to go beyond accepted frameworks toward the development of democratic curricula. In parts I and II of the book, through teaching and research articles, children's writing, parents' and teachers' voices, and burning issues, we have attempted to encourage participants in greater understandings of themselves, the students they teach, and the broader cultural framework within which teachers live and work. On a personal note, it is our hope that all teachers and students, at all levels of education, may move from a local to a more universal location within themselves, extending to other places to truly become citizens of the world.

The third and final part of the book attempts to move toward a pedagogy of hope and school change, in order to incorporate change for social action. Without the means of becoming agents for social change, "good" teachers may lose hope and eventually leave the profession or remain in their classrooms as "mechanical teachers." But is not the most difficult and imaginative work one of putting theory into practice? Chapter 9 begins with one preservice student's experience at trying to create and imagine change for positive social action within his high school classroom. The chapter culminates with a teacher educator's lived experience of attempting to model community building in the preservice classroom and beyond.

These two lived experiences illuminate the benefit of moving beyond the deconstruction of teachers' work in schools in order to proceed toward a pedagogy of hope and school change. In this way, perhaps all individuals can find ways to respect and to be invested in those issues fundamental to all human beings. To be respectful allows for improved lines of communication in the face of difference and diversity, moving beyond tolerance to acknowledgment and hopefully toward acceptance.

The challenge and the invitation of this book has been to actively engage educators, including children, in essential matters: curricular activities that can assist them in exchanging educational scripts that make them uncomfortable for newer, more innovative and inclusive practices that may lead to the development of their own voices. It is our hope that all teachers and students might truly have opportunities to "see with their own eyes and feel with their own hearts."

Chapter Nine

Equity: Beyond
Difference and Diversity

The true value of a human being is determined primarily by the measure and the sense in which he has attained liberation from the self.

—Albert Einstein (*Einstein: A Portrait*)

Stories of oppression are embedded within the larger structures of society—the political, historical, social, and economic conditions in which oppression has its roots and may continue to evolve. These stories are sometimes dominant and sometimes submerged, but they are always context dependent and always have universal themes, such as those related to issues of power, control, access, participation, centralization, and decentralization and tensions between the rights of individual members within society and the common good.

While there has been a significant shift in issues of social justice over the last several decades, there remains a need on the part of all individuals to look continuously and closely at one's own participation in matters of social justice. Perhaps by beginning with one's own lived experiences, constructed within one's own biographic and subjective geographies, it may be possible to be truly aware of the barriers and boundaries of oppression and the needless pain and suffering that these obstacles inflict across personal, national, and international borders. The task of recognizing these injustices requires empathy and the deepening of one's own understanding in order to identify the myriad of issues that might constitute oppression in all forms. What follows is one teacher's attempt to put theory into practice in the context of his high school teaching experience.

A Teacher's Response to Intolerance in Our Schools

Much of my focus in my teaching this year and in previous years has been to try to respond to the racism and intolerance that has existed throughout history and connect those moments to how these issues play out in our present society and in our classrooms. I have specifically focused on teaching about the Holocaust and other genocides in the twentieth century. I have noticed that my teaching of this topic comes from a very personal place. My personal background has been a substantial source of my motivation for teaching. In addition, I have noticed that while teaching such a personal issue, I have opened myself and my students up to exploring issues that can be both very painful and very rewarding. I would like to focus my burning issue essay on sharing the personal experience that prompted me to teach about intolerance and examining some of my experiences teaching about this in my practicums this year.

Prior to Grade 11, the experience of cultural alienation had never come my way. 1 was sent to school in a safe environment of a private Jewish school, where I was taught to cherish my identity and the identities of other cultures. When I was in Grade 10, I entered the world of the public school. It was a major culture clash. It took about six months for me to adjust to the experience of blending with other cultures. Because I was at an arts high school, I was in an intense program to study theatre. Looking back, I believe that because my peers and I had a common goal and focus, we began to respect each other as actors and colleagues. As a result, we became more open to the idea that each person came from a specific background and had something unique to share with the entire group.

My feeling of relative comfort with being in a public school completely changed in a matter of moments. I was sitting in an O.A.C. law class, and we were studying about a hate literature clause. This is the clause which says that if hate is being promoted against a specific group, it is not permissible to publish or distribute the material. The topic of the Holocaust was used as an example of why neo-Nazi literature is often banned in Canada. One student raised his hand and said; " Why do Jews have to get together and cry every year about something that happened fifty years ago, and who knows if it even happened anyway?" Those words were ringing in my ears and I felt my blood boiling, I waited for the teacher to respond. She did not. I was the only Jewish student in my class and the other students were mainly white, with a few other cultures represented. At first I was furious with the kid who said it, because I had learned about the Holocaust first-hand. My mother never met anyone from her parents' family because they were all killed because they were hated for being different.

After the class, I thought about it and realized that I was more angry at the teacher than the student. The student seemed to say it as if he knew nothing about the Holocaust. The complacency of the other students suggested that they too were ignorant about the topic. But the teacher had no excuse. Even if the teacher did not know much about the issue, she had a responsibility to react with decency and sensitivity. Because I was very upset, I went and spoke with family about the issue, and they too were upset. They suggested that I go in and speak with the teacher about it. I did say that I felt very uncomfortable, and during the next class the teacher showed a video on the Holocaust. While that was a start, and it made some of the other students think, the teacher did not process the roots of racism with the students and never apologized for remaining silent.

Looking back on this experience, I realize that I was very lucky to have been a fairly emotionally stable child with a good family support system. Without this, I could have either lashed out and gotten into a physical confrontation with the other student or I could have internalized this painful experience and it could have alienated me from my teachers and peers, leading to depression or possibly even substance abuse or suicide. Worst of all, I could have felt tremendous shame from my culture and could have been afraid to openly practice it. Fortunately, none of these things happened to me, but they could have easily happened to another student in the exact same situation. What still remains with me today is the silence of the teacher. The cultural alienation that happened to me and the mistrust of teachers that I developed all could have been avoided if the teacher had reacted appropriately by defending and acknowledging all cultures in the classroom.

In the years after this experience, what has occurred to me is that the racist comments that come up in classrooms are often rooted in ignorance. Thus, I decided that I would take it upon myself as a teacher to find ways to respond to the ignorance through effective education and fill the silence. I decided that it would be important to teach about the Holocaust in a creative and engaging way. Too often these issues are only addressed through a textbook.

In my first practicum at Earl Grey, I taught a mini course on the Holocaust to Grade 8 students. In preparing to teach, I planned that I would use audiovisual resources, literature, and personal anecdotes to connect students to this mass human tragedy. While my focus was the European Holocaust, I broadened my topic to include the Rwandan, Cambodian, Armenian, and Yugoslavian genocides from this century.

I began the unit by staging a role play for students on discrimination, focusing on how they would feel in the situation where they were being discriminated against. I followed this with a slide presentation focusing on the European Holocaust, also referring to Rwanda, Armenia, and Cambodia. I stressed that the twentieth century has been one of the most bloody and discussed the roots of racism. I accompanied the slide presentation with music from the Holocaust in order to set the mood.

What I observed was that the students took the subject quite seriously. I found that the music and dim lights and the role play helped to engage them and served as a much-needed mental set for this topic. I found it challenging to remain nonemotional because of the personal nature of this topic. I found that it worked to share my personal story with my students. I told them that I had lost a lot of my family on my mother's side in the Holocaust. I told my students that my family was killed and I never got a chance to meet them. I told them how they were killed only because they were hated for the fact that they were different. The class then got into a discussion on multiculturalism and the importance of living in an inclusive society.

At one moment, a girl shared with the class that she had some Muslim friends who had said that Jewish people were bad people. I found it very challenging to deal with this comment. I explained that the point of this class was to demonstrate the harmful effects of hate against specific groups. I also said that I would be willing to discuss it further with her individually after class.

I also noticed that as a teacher, I felt I had to detach at this moment and let go of my gut instinct to respond emotionally. What I learned from this experience is that it is important for teachers to be personal with students when it is related to a topic they are teaching. However, they should proceed with caution. I learned that when addressing issues of racism, teachers should expect some racist and homophobic comments from students. It is important to address those on the spot without getting into a power struggle with a student.

It is also important for teachers to realize that in these situations, students often get their prior knowledge from their parents and other students. Therefore, it is very important to not blame them and to simply work hard to correct the mistaken racist comment. I also learned that there is hardly a more rewarding experience for both a teacher and a student than working through issues in racism.

I believe that an essential part of anti-racist education is to refer to the mistakes that societies have made in history. While I was teaching these topics, I found that the issue was very personal for me, and I was able to use that to my advantage. Most of all, I have found that teachers have a strong reason for being teachers. They are often emotional and ideological. I look forward to continuing my journey of attempting to fill the silence that led to my experience of cultural alienation in a classroom.

While this burning issue essay speaks mostly to issues of racial and cultural intolerance, it may be pertinent to all forms of intolerance, some of which have been explored within the pages of this book. It may also be important to note that learning tolerance is only part of the journey along the path of self-recognition, self-respect, and respect for others. How will we know when we have arrived? Perhaps the movement from tolerance to acceptance will be the sign by which we will know that it is time to begin again, to ensure that no one's voice is missing and that all voices have been listened to and acted upon. This is equity, where everyone is included regardless of age, orientation, class, or race.

To put this into practice may be the demanding part of teachers' work, but it is also the rich work of teachers demonstrated through the following reflection and accompanying photograph.

Debbie Pushor: The Rich Work of Teachers

One of the things I've come to see as central to my work as a teacher educator is the collaborative exploration with preservice teachers of beliefs about teaching, learning, and children. This exploration enables us to reflect on, articulate, challenge, affirm, and symbolize our beliefs, both individually and collectively. It enables us to build community as a group sharing a course and to use this process of exploration as a way to talk about and imagine building community in classrooms with children.

This year, in a course called Integrated Curriculum, I used a children's book by Byrd Baylor, *The Table Where Rich People Sit* (1999), as a way

to frame this process of exploration. In the story, a little girl calls her family to a meeting around their homemade kitchen table to discuss money—the fact that their family doesn't have enough of it. Through the conversation, her family helps her see how rich they are and that their kitchen table is a table where rich people sit. Playing off of their conversation, our class discussed the things that made us rich as a community and the ways in which we wanted to live together throughout the course to ensure that those riches were realized. Having developed our "classroom creed," we began to talk about how we each might develop such a creed in our own classrooms. As we read Ayers's book *To Teach: The Journey of a Teacher* (2001), our conversation moved to what we see the rich work of teachers as being. It was then that I introduced the idea of making our own table "where rich people sit."

In a common space in our education building, under a beautiful arched window, there sits a long narrow table—usually surrounded by students engaged in shared project work. Since it is a communal table, I proposed that each student depict on a ceramic tile what she or he saw the rich work of teaching to be and that together we grout the tiles onto the table, giving it a new surface—and a new meaning. The preservice teachers loved the idea and took ownership of it. In each class period during the course, four students shared their completed tiles, talking about the words, symbols, and images on their tiles and sharing their hopes and dreams for the kind of classrooms they would create with children and the lives they would live as teachers. This sharing time was an emotional part of each class, a time in which we got to know one another in deeper and more meaningful ways. When all the tiles were complete, we spent a number of days gluing, grouting, and sealing our tiles on the table. When it was finished, we held a celebration. We talked about how a table such as this one could become a central gathering place in a classroom—a place of connection, a place to celebrate, a place to solve problems and resolve conflicts, a place to come together in community.

"The table where rich people sit" is now back in its place under the window in our education building. Each time I walk past it, it reinforces for me the importance of creating experiences in classrooms which bond a group of people together. The experience of creating the table brought our class together in a unique way; it defined and connected us as a group. It also gave us a concrete and visual symbol of what it is we believe in. Each time we glance at the table, we are reminded to stay focused on the rich work of teachers.

Perhaps this lived experience suggests that effective teaching depends most fundamentally on human relationships. The authors believe that these human relationships can only be fostered in a community that values and respects both differences and similarities in the spirit of critical inquiry. This is the rich work of teaching and learning, to be able to suspend one's own judgments, agendas, and biases in order to fully recognize that while the work of teachers begins with ourselves it ends by encouraging students and all members of society to take up this rich and demanding work. Perhaps this means to reenvision a more democratic society, one in which there are more members who attain liberation from self in order to become agents of positive social change.

REFERENCES

Ayers, W. 2001. *To Teach: The Journey of a Teacher*. 2nd ed. New York: Teachers College Press.

Baylor, B., and P. Parnall. 1999. *The Table Where Rich People Sit*. New York: Simon & Schuster.

n.a. 1984. *Einstein: A Portrait*. Corte Madera, Calif.: Pomegranate Artbooks.

Index

About the Authors

Karyn Cooper is an assistant professor of teacher education, literacy, language, and culture at the Ontario Institute for Studies in Education of the University of Toronto. Her research focuses on the sociocultural dimensions of literacy and teacher education.

Robert E. White has taught extensively in public school systems across Canada and is currently assistant professor of inclusion at St. Francis Xavier University in Nova Scotia. Research interests include critical aspects of literacy, learning, and leadership.